THE
TWISTED
FLORIN

THE
TWISTED
FLORIN

by

Stella Clare Marsh

UNIFORM

UNIFORM

This edition first published in 2016 by Uniform
an imprint of Unicorn Publishing Group LLP

101 Wardour Street
London
W1F 0UG
www.unicornpublishing.org

ISBN 978-1-910500-58-3

Printed and Bound in Great Britain

CONTENTS

DEDICATION

To my
Aunt Barbara Mott,
with love.

Elizabeth Lucas Harrison MBE was the sculptor who created the Royal Air Forces Escaping Society memorial. The text reads:

'On the 21st June 1981 this plaque was dedicated to the countless brave men and women of enemy occupied countries who, during World War Two (1939-45) without thought of danger to themselves, helped 2803 aircrew of the Royal Air Force and Commonwealth Air Forces to escape and return to this country and so continue the struggle for freedom. Many paid with their lives; many more endured the degradation of concentration camps. Their names are remembered in equal honour with those who were spared to fight a longer battle. To mark its debt of gratitude, The Royal Air Forces Escaping Society erected this memorial as a lasting tribute and also to serve as an inspiration to future generations.'

Here follows part of the lesson read at the dedication service at the Central Church of the Royal Air Force at Saint Clement Danes in London:

'For I was an hungred, and ye gave me meat: I was thirsty, and ye gave me drink: I was a stranger, and ye took me in:'

Matthew 25:35
(King James version)

ACKNOWLEDGEMENTS

First and foremost, a massive thank you to all my family, near and far and across four generations, for their contributions; from Aunty Barbara's memories to Daniel Mott's school project. I am grateful to each and every one of you for all the many ways in which you have assisted me with this mammoth task. I shall always be especially grateful to my husband Andrew; for his constant help and support.

It saddens me that Elizabeth Lucas Harrison, MBE, is no longer with us to read my completed book. I owe a huge debt of gratitude for her constant assistance throughout this long journey, and for starting me off with a gift of the book *Safe Houses are Dangerous*, written by her good friend Helen Long.

Thanks also to Martyn Cox of The Secret WW2 Learning Network for your help in so many directions, particularly the access to your amazing interviews; your advice and assistance has been invaluable.

Joel Diggle, thank you for giving me so much of your time and for sharing your vast knowledge and your resources so generously. The artwork provided by your friend Geoff Pleasance is outstanding.

Thank you Kevin O'Kelly, for all your help with the text; it was, as ever, a pleasure to work with you and your knowledge of grammar and syntax has been exceptionally useful.

To my newfound friend Tanya Bruce-Lockhart (Guy Lockhart's daughter), I really appreciate all the help you have given me in bringing your father's wartime achievements to light and for allowing me access to your treasured papers.

Thank you Ryan Gearing and Bridget Neale at Unicorn Publishing Group for helping me, step-by-step, to bring this book to fruition.

The staff of The Imperial War Museum gave me so much help as I trawled through the many boxes containing the RAFES records and the private papers of Patrick Martin-Smith.

So many more people have helped me along the way. My thanks in particular to the following:

Bob Body of The Tempsford Veterans and Relatives Association for his help with details of the Special Duties squadrons operating out of Tempsford; Bob Frost and Andrée Dumon (Nadine) for permission to quote from their transcripts; Rev.

Bruce Lyons for permission to quote from his sermon at a meeting of the Royal Air Forces Escaping Society in Brussels celebrating the anniversary of the setting up of the Comet Line; Caroline Wyatt for her BBC report from Auschwitz at the end of January 2015, which gave me the courage to delve more deeply into the horrors of Ravensbrück and Mauthausen; Dr.Christopher Warne for his help at The University of Sussex; David Furniss and Felicia Ruperti for their sterling work translating text from French to English; Professor David Guss for his generous sharing of knowledge about Gavi; David Harrison for comprehensive information about André Simon; Philippe Meert, Mark Crame, Michele Heck, Edouard Renière and Victor Schutters for their help in piecing together the facts about Alex Nitelet; Geoff Cowling for his assistance with information on the British Consulate in Barcelona; Guy Revell of the RAF Museum; Jenny Schmidt, Bob Parrott's daughter, for her generous access to her father's papers; Joe Dible for sharing his extraordinary knowledge of WW2 aircraft; John Clinch for all his help; Judy Yeoman, Allan Yeoman's daughter, for sharing her knowledge; Keith Janes for his website and book; Ken Marshall for enhancing my knowledge of Whitleys; Margaret Wadman of Christ's Hospital; Martin Wallman for bringing old video and audio tapes to life; Martyn Bell of The Secret WW2 Learning Network for his generous help with information about Raymond Fassin; Nicolas Livingstone and Peter Perkins for information about Operation WHITSUN; Peter Osborne for permission to quote from *Blue Skies and Dark Nights; the autobiography of Bill Randle*; Pierre Tillet for his infiltrations list and personal help; Reginald Byron of the Tangmere Museum; Roger Stanton of ELMS for his time on the telephone and permission to quote from ELMS published text; Roy Tebbutt of the Carpetbagger Aviation Museum; Serge Tilly for sharing his knowledge of the Resistance; Steve Andrews for his knowledge of 148 Squadron; Steve Cooney of Tempsford Museum; Steven Kippax for giving me access to the Special Operations Executive forum; Suzey Ott and Tim Hutchins for their help with the 'Pitch and Toss' adventure; and Michael Dunning, trustee of the Brunswick Club, for supplying me with so much useful information about the club.

FOREWORD

I am delighted to be given the opportunity to write a foreword to The Twisted Florin. It is a fascinating record of exceptional deeds, enormous courage and great fortitude and reminds us that, even in the midst of evil and adversity, the human spirit still shines through and ultimately triumphs.

For those Allied aircrew flying deep into enemy held territory by day and night during the Second World War, the knowledge that being shot down did not necessarily mean capture and a prisoner of war camp – that there were brave men and women willing to risk all to help their escape – was a powerful motivation. And over 2800 airmen did escape and were successfully returned to the UK, to continue the fight for freedom and help ensure eventual victory.

Squadron Leader John Mott's story is all the more remarkable – he was one of the very few to return to the fight first as an Evader from France and subsequently, after an all too brief tour with the Special Duties squadrons, as an Escaper, traversing enemy held territory to once again return to duty.

The price paid was frequently high for those who assisted escapees. The debt that the Royal Air Force owed was very well recognised at the time, both officially and by individual airmen; it was also recognised after the war. But as the generation passes for whom these experiences were lived at first hand, it is vital that we continue to record for new generations the memory of those people and their incredible deeds. I congratulate Stella Marsh on what she has achieved with The Twisted Florin, a work of both historical record and personal recollection. She has helped keep alive a vital part of the Royal Air Force's history, and helped provide fresh inspiration for the Royal Air Force of today.

Air Chief Marshal Sir Stephen Hillier KCB CBE DFC ADC MA RAF
Chief of the Air Staff
September 2016

Birmingham

ENGLAND

NORTH
SEA

HOLLAND

Rotterdam

LONDON

Bristol

Dover

Dunkerque

Dortmund

St Omer

BRUSSELS

BELGIUM

GERMANY

Frankfurt

ENGLISH CHANNEL

Dieppe

Rouen

Reims

Metz

MILITARY ZONE

Caen

PARIS

Strasbourg

Brest

ALSACE

Lorient

Rennes

O C C U P I E D   Z O N E

Orléans

Dijon

Tours

Berne

Nantes

Issoudun

Le
Fay

SWITZERLAND

Poitiers

Chateauroux

La Rochelle

Vichy

Limoges

Lyons

ITALY

BAY
OF
BISCAY

F R A N C E

Grenoble

Turin

Bordeaux

F R E E   Z O N E

DEMARCATION LINE

Nimes

Nice

Monaco

Toulouse

Marseilles

Éze

Pamplona

Toulon

MEDITERRANEAN SEA

SPAIN

Perpignan

Latour-
de-Carol

Zaragoza

Barcelona

**FRANCE
AND ITALY 1942/43**

...eas under Italian
...cupation, November
...42–September 1943

0   50   100   150   200

MILES

ITALY AND
THE BALKANS
1943/45

PREFACE

When I was a young child my Grandmother told me that she was the luckiest woman in England. She explained that her husband came home from the trenches at the end of the First World War and her three sons eventually arrived home from their duty in the three Services throughout the Second World War with all their limbs intact. Although I was born in the middle of the Second World War, I was too young to have any memories of that time, so it was many years before I had any real comprehension of why she considered herself so lucky.

After the war none of the brothers spoke much about their experiences except when speaking to one another. Both my cousin Judie and I were in the habit of making ourselves as invisible as we could and listening in to some of these conversations. I can picture clearly a few precious times when Uncle John would stay with us because he needed to be in London for a meeting or function. My father and uncle would be companionably completing the Daily Telegraph crossword while my mother worked her way through a pile of ironing. I would sit very quietly on the stairs and listen to their reminiscences. Likewise Judie would listen to John and Pip when they were planning family outings in Petersfield, where both families lived for a while.

The most extraordinary story was that of Uncle John, evader and escaper. However, he was adamant that he did not wish anyone to put an account of his experiences into print. He had a friend who was secretary to the Goons and who thought when they disbanded, it was a wonderful opportunity to document all of these – he would not countenance this at that time.

When the adventures of Douglas Bader became an exciting book and then a film I chatted to Uncle John about how wonderful it was. His response dampened my enthusiasm very effectively; he told me that when eight Spitfire pilots were shot down over the Pas de Calais whilst on a bomber escort mission known as CIRCUS 68, four of them died, three were taken prisoner of war, and one evaded capture and was brought safely back to England in spite of losing an eye. Uncle John later flew this man, Alex Nitelet, back to France to act as a wireless operator and guide for the PAT line. I was told that he was the true hero whose story should have been told. Consequently, I have researched the story of this brave man and included as much as I can find alongside Uncle John's exploits.

All three brothers attended Christ's Hospital school and were members of the Officer Training Corps (OTC). They served throughout the Second World War, as did most of their classmates; each of the three brothers choosing a different service. In about 1990, all three brothers arranged to attend Old Blues Day at Christ's Hospital School and visit John's grandson, Andrew, at the school. This was a really special day; I drove them to the school and trailed behind them as Andrew gave them the guided tour. During the course of the day they were approached to write an account of their wartime experiences for an author who was compiling a book and they were persuaded that this would be useful heritage. Judie painstakingly typed up Pip's account and I did the same for Mervyn. John had recently acquired an Amstrad computer and keyed in his own story. The book proved to be of little consequence, using the barest minimum of their accounts. However, the precious documents written by the brothers formed the original basis for my research.

Fortunately, Uncle John's attitude changed around this time. When I asked if he would consider letting me write a full version for family history, he told me that I could certainly do so but only after his death and on the condition that I took the time to include the very useful contribution of his two brothers in the other two services. He also pointed out that they were simply following the example of their father in the First World War.

When Uncle John died in 2002, some members of his immediate family particularly wished for the story to be told by a specific writer and so I shelved the research I had compiled, not knowing then that this plan would not come to fruition.

I have retired now and with my aunt's blessing have spent hundreds of hours reading books, researching, and talking to relations to collect the relevant facts. The journey has been long and difficult and only the inherited Mott family determination has kept me from settling for what was initially available. The book is the result of a determined personal mission inspired by the love I have always had for my uncle and aunt. Their inspiration has kept me going while tracking down surviving veterans and gaining the enthusiastic and generous support of a network of leading historians, researchers, and writers, each of whose specialities and expertise pertain to different aspects of my narrative. I am now able to fulfil the agreement made so long ago while the three brothers and my Grandfather are still within living memory.

1

FROM THE FIRST WORLD WAR TO THE SECOND

Arthur Mott was born in Notting Hill London in 1884, the seventh of eight children. In April 1912, Arthur was a clerk in the Westminster Bank in Stony Stratford in Buckinghamshire when he met and married a nurse, Florence Barnes, from Tingewick. Their first son, Mervyn Gerard, was born in March 1915 in Tingewick and the family then moved to Guildford in Surrey. In those happy months before war was declared, Arthur and Florence saw in the New Year by dancing under the Tunsgate clock in Guildford High Street. By the time Arnold John Mott was born in May 1916, Arthur, now aged 31, had enlisted with the London Regiment (Artists' Rifles).

On 19th March 1917, Arthur embarked at Southampton and travelled to Le Havre to join his unit fighting in the trenches in Rouen. He had two weeks leave in August, returning to Rouen on 2nd September, but by 5th November was suffering from recurring trench fever. This showed on his records as PUO; Pyrexia of Unknown Origin, a medical term usually applied to trench fever. He was invalided back to England on 18th November and posted back to Rouen on 10th March 1918. Florence and the two boys moved back to her parents' home in Tingewick, where her third son, Percival Eric (Pip), was born on 17th April. Arthur was discharged as no longer fit for war service at Romford on 11th December, 1918.

Arthur's father Herbert was the tenth of thirteen children, whose oldest brother, George, had emigrated to Australia in 1857. All five of George's sons served in the First World War. Their mother, Elizabeth, was widowed before the start of the war and her youngest son, Arthur Ernest Percival, died on a training flight off the coast of Scotland in December 1917 at the age of 22. Even at that young age he had a remarkable service record, which included building a wireless station at Gazza and he had proved himself a hero when travelling on the Transylvania, saving four lives when she was sunk by a submarine in May 1917. The oldest brother, John Eldred, also had a remarkable service record; he was awarded the Military Cross whilst serving in Pozières, in the Somme. He was wounded and captured at Bullecourt (the second line of German trenches) on 11th April 1917, suffering wounds in his neck, back and stomach and losing two fingers of one hand; he later became the first Australian to escape from a German Prisoner of War camp. He escaped in November 1917 and returned to the front where he was awarded a Bar to his Military Cross for conspicuous gallantry and devotion to duty on 8th August 1918, during the advance on Proyart. In 1919 he received the MBE from King George V.

The extended Mott family corresponded frequently and while they were growing up Arthur's three sons were very aware of his own military service and that of the Australian branch of the family. John followed in his father's footsteps and created a family tree using the copious detailed notes made by his grandfather. Through most of the 1920s, the family lived in Rotherfield House which later became part of The Royal Latin School in Buckingham and it was from there that Mervyn, John and Pip went to Christ's Hospital boarding school in Horsham. Life at home was under a strict regime, with good behaviour and impeccable manners high on the agenda. Arthur was a keen gardener and beekeeper; Mervyn in particular was also very interested in both of these pursuits. Meals were taken at a large dining table and the boys were under strict instructions not to reach in front of each other to grab what they wanted. Arthur built a clockwork railway system to run around the table, with stopping points in front of each place. Everything from jam to pickle was carried in the wagons and the three brothers all had fond memories of this delightful system.

Further back in history, some of London's dignitaries had persuaded Henry VIII to bring hundreds of poor children off the streets of the city and into a new school housed in the empty Greyfriars monastery. Henry died before this came to fruition, so it was Edward VI who eventually signed the royal charter and thus founded the unique Christ's Hospital School in 1552. The school flourished through the centuries and is richly endowed. In early 1902, the school purchased a large farm and moved from

THREE BROTHERS AT HOME — MOTT FAMILY COLLECTION

London to an enormous twelve hundred acre site in Horsham. The architects brought many of the features of the London site to Horsham and included the original spelling of the school motto on the cloister arch. It must have seemed strange to the pupils through the years as they marched under the arch to see the words 'Fear God, love the Brotherhood, Honor the King'. Families did not need to be poor to send their children to Christ's Hospital, just from professions that were not well paid. Arthur Mott was a bank clerk, so educating his three sons at the very best of schools would not otherwise have been in his reach. Each of the three boys had a donating governor, who had the right to present a suitable pupil in return for a financial donation. In John's case the donating governor was his uncle, Walter John Barnes, whose daughter Honor had travelled from Durban, Natal to be educated at the Christ's Hospital Girls Grammar School in Hertford.

On his first day at the school, John would have been taken to Horsham wearing his normal clothes, alighting from the train at the school's own railway station called West Horsham Christ's Hospital. Assuming that his father had accompanied him, he would have taken John's clothes home once he had been dressed in the unique school uniform. Little had changed since Tudor times; the uniform consisted of a long, belted blue coat, knee breeches, a white shirt with no buttons, mustard coloured socks, and a belt known as a girdle. The term dates took up nine months of the year, during which time life was spent almost entirely within the vast acreage that made up the whole of the site. Some of this was out of bounds to the boys but they still had extensive playing fields and areas where they could explore when they were not required to be in a specific place in their structured lives. Life was made easier for John by the fact that his brother, Mervyn, just a year older than him, was already established at the school when John commenced his education there. Mervyn went exploring with his young brother one Sunday afternoon; John wanted to pick a bulrush growing on the banks of a pond. Unfortunately John lost his balance and fell in. His big brother now had to bring him back to school across about seven fields and hand him over to Matron. Mervyn was sent to the Headmaster for a severe dressing down, while John was given a nice hot bath and regaled with cake for the rest of the afternoon. The next time John fell into icy, cold water he would be fortunate to have a friend on hand but there would be no hot bath or cake in those grim circumstances…

A prominent feature outside the dining room at Christ's Hospital is the War Memorial inscribed 'Sons of this House who gave their lives for their Country

1914-1918. The memorial contains three hundred and seventy eight names. The dining room itself was vast and contained one of the largest paintings in the world; created by Antonio Verrio to commemorate the foundation of the Royal Mathematical School in 1673, it is simply known as 'the Verrio'. Over eight hundred people were seated for each meal.

All three brothers were in Barnes B, which had the motto *Umbra fugit, manet res* – 'The shadow flies, the situation remains'. Each house had its own table but the fifty plus pupils were seated in order of seniority, so the brothers would not have been within speaking distance of each other. The house captain was seated at the head of the table and the newest intake at the bottom. These youngest members of the house would have had the task of waiting on their seniors. There was plenty of fresh produce from the farm on site but the food was not remembered with any pleasure. The brothers' memories of mealtimes at the school they called 'Housey' were of anonymous stews served from vast vats and the discipline that every scrap of food on the plate must be eaten regardless of the taste. All this and many other aspects of their schooling were a solid preparation for what this generation of boys were to face within a few short years.

All activities outside the classroom were organised by the senior boys; seniority was determined by year of entry and the rank of a senior boy commanded respect from his juniors. This was another aspect of Housey life that was a valuable preparation for wartime life in the services.

In the large dormitories there were twenty four unsprung beds with basic horsehair mattresses laid out with military precision. There were washing facilities and lavatories at the ends of the room and a monitor would stay in the room to study for a while after lights out each night. At weekends the monitor would read a bedtime story to the boys listening in the dark. When Pip visited John's grandson at the school, decades after the brothers' time there, it looked so familiar that Pip just had to check to see if the horsehair mattresses were still in place.

The tuck cupboard was situated outside the dayroom and was unlocked for a couple of hours each day. All food from outside the school had to be stored in the cupboard. Florence Mott made wonderful fruit cakes for her sons; there is no record of how long they lasted. All three were amused in later life by their shared memory of waiting for the cupboard to be opened, each of them with a teaspoon in hand so that they could share a tin of condensed milk.

THREE BROTHERS AT SCHOOL — MOTT FAMILY COLLECTION

SAILING TOY BOATS ON HOLIDAY FROM SCHOOL — A GOOD PRACTICE FOR WHAT
WAS TO COME? — MOTT FAMILY COLLECTION

All the teachers at the school were Oxbridge graduates and the most able pupils were prepared for entry to these two universities. Only these pupils were taught French. The second language taught throughout the rest of the school was German. Religion was at the heart of the school. There were prayers at each end of the day and Grace and a scripture reading before meals.

Sport was a major feature of school life, rugby in particular, with an emphasis on playing the game well rather than winning at all costs. The dayroom played host to other leisure pursuits; cribbage and chess whiled away many hours for Mervyn but bridge was John's game of choice.

The two brothers were in the library one day looking through the school notes in *The Blue*, the school magazine, when they came across an entry in Vol. LV, No. 4 that fascinated both of them. It was about a visit from a previous pupil called James Charles Henry Tavendale, who had attended Christ's Hospital from 1916 to 1922:

> 'JCH Tavendale (Lamb B, 1916-1922), now an officer in the RAF, swooped down upon us out of the fog in his plane on 1st March, and after a successful landing near the cinder path to the Two-Mile Ash Road, and, we hope, an equally successful lunch in Hall, departed again successfully before a crowded "house" after the steeplechase.'

In 1930, a block of science workshops and a new quadrangle were added to the school. The donors had a particular wish to educate the boys in scientific agriculture so that they might have new opportunities in the development of the resources of the British Empire. Experimental work was carried on under glass on the flat roof. Aquatic plants were grown for study in ornamental waters in the quadrangle. Mervyn took part in this special botany work and John took an interest in his brother's activities with the plants. Who could have known then just how useful John's knowledge of botany would later prove to be, when he would have to forage for survival during the Second World War?

It was also in 1930 that a significant event triggered John's ambition to fly. An Old Blue, Barnes Wallace, played a major role in the design of the R100 airship that had its base at Cardigan aerodrome. During the First World War, German airships had rained bombs on London, killing many innocent women and children as well as causing great damage. The pupils at Christ's Hospital were far too young to have any memories of this, and the fact that a German airship was due to pass over Horsham caused great excitement. On Saturday 26th April, the Graf Zeppelin was on its way to land beside the R100 that was moored on its mast at Cardigan. The flight was timed to fly low over Wembley, where the cup final was being played. Once it had passed over Brighton at sixteen minutes past three, it was only a short distance to Horsham, where all the pupils were gathered in the large quadrangle. This was the moment when John first announced that he was going to be a pilot. The Wembley Stadium flyover was not an unqualified success, because many of the men attending the FA cup final between Huddersfield Town and Arsenal had memories of the German airships during the war, and they shook their fists at the huge structure flying so close above their heads.

Just weeks later, on 14th May, Flight Lieutenant James Charles Henry Tavendale of 20 Squadron, flying Bristol Fighter F4562, crashed at Ali Musjid near his base at Peshawar in India and was killed alongside his co-pilot, Henry John Chapell.

The boys were taught that the British Empire was the greatest force for good in the modern world, bringing peace and the rule of law to lawless places. For centuries many Old Blues had lived and worked in far-off places, developing the local economies and generally raising standards. On leaving school Pip chose to head for India to work, intending to make his fortune and then return to England after a couple of decades.

MOTT BROTHERS AT HOME SUMMER 1937
MOTT FAMILY COLLECTION

One interest that the brothers shared was the OTC, the Officer Training Corps, which had been founded in 1904. Here they dressed in uniforms like those worn in WW1 and there was an extensive armoury; pictures from the time show the pupils on parade with fixed bayonets. During the first battle of Monte Cassino, Pip was to experience fighting with fixed bayonets under instructions not to fire within the walls. Initially, every effort was made to preserve this ancient place but, by the time the fourth Battle of Monte Cassino took place, it had been reduced to rubble and lost to posterity. One of the features of their training was that they were taken to the far boundaries of the school grounds and then left to find their own way back. The incentive was to make it back to the dining room in time for tea, or else go hungry. All of this was to stand John in good stead in the coming war, on his solo expeditions across the Pyrénées then later up into the Julian Alps.

At the end of their time at Christ's Hospital, there was a special leaving service, in which each boy was presented with a Bible as a gift from the governors before assembling before the altar while the Headmaster read 'The Charge':

'I charge you never to forget the great benefits that you have received in this place, and in time to come according to your means, to do all that you can to enable others to enjoy the same advantage; and remember that you carry with you, wherever you go, the good name of Christ's Hospital. May God Almighty bless you in your ways and keep you in the knowledge of his love now and forever.'

By the time the brothers left school, the Mott family home was in Wallington in Surrey. Pip left home on 26th February, 1938, travelling First Class on SS The City of Cairo en route to Calcutta. Over the following years, he would have a number of sea journeys but none of these would be in any such luxury.

John began work as a bank clerk in London, and he soon met a girl called Whyn Bignall who worked at Winsor and Newton, a company supplying fine art materials. They met together regularly after work and John took a fancy to the gingerbread cake served in their favourite tea room. He eventually persuaded the owner to part with the recipe. His mother was happy to cook it for him and this cake became a firm favourite; it is still known in the family as 'Arnold's gingerbread', and the recipe is copied from my Grandmother's recipe book (with the original imperial measurements):

Arnold's Gingerbread

Ingredients

12 ozs Flour

12 ozs Syrup

4 ozs Butter

3 ozs Demerara Sugar

3 teaspoons Ground Ginger

1 Teaspoon Bicarbonate of Soda

1 and a half gills Milk

Cream Butter and Sugar together, add Syrup and Milk. Mix Flour, Ginger and Soda together then add to the other ingredients: turn onto a greased Swiss Roll tin or ordinary baking tin, previously lined with greased paper: put into a very hot oven for five minutes, then turn the gas very low and leave undisturbed for 55 minutes. *DO NOT OPEN OVEN DOOR MEANWHILE.* A cloth put over the cake when taken from the oven keeps it moist. If liked a handful of Sultanas can be added to the dry mixture.

2

FROM BOMBER PILOT
TO EVADER

QUALIFIED PILOT
MOTT FAMILY COLLECTION

On the morning of 7th September 1939, Mervyn and John (the groom and best man, respectively), dressed in top hats and tails, were all set to leave for the church with their parents when John was 'called to the colours'. He had enlisted in the Royal Air Force Volunteer Reserve on 1st January 1938 and had begun his training as a pilot at the Reserve Flying Training School at Redhill aerodrome on 1st June 1939. Now he had to abandon the wedding and leave immediately for basic training followed by further flying training at Cambridge aerodrome.

In April 1940, he transferred to Shawbury in Shropshire to learn to fly twin-engine aircraft, during which time he had his first experience of war. On 27th June, a German intruder aircraft dropped a stick of bombs across the barracks, one of which landed outside his bedroom window, covering him and his bed with shards of glass.

In July 1940, John transferred to Operational Training at Kinloss in Scotland, prior to posting to 78 (Heavy Bomber) Squadron at Dishforth, Yorkshire in October 1940, to fly Whitleys for bombing operations against enemy targets.

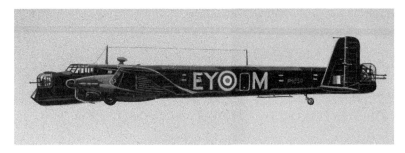

WHITLEY BOMBER
ARTWORK — BY GEOFF PLEASANCE

The Whitley, the RAF's first 'heavy' bomber, was used as the first night bomber by Bomber Command, operating at night; the Wellington and Hampden bombers operated mainly during daylight hours. The construction was all metal and its main characteristic was a peculiar nose-down attitude in flight.

Giving a talk to some schoolchildren many years later, John described the Whitley thus:

'The type of aeroplane that we used for bombing raids during the war was quite peculiar; it didn't really look like an aeroplane but was a large box affair with two engines. The Whitley had a maximum speed of 105 miles an hour and carried about 6000lbs of bombs, shall we say six to eight 500lb bombs. Compare that to the end of the war; they were using 10,000lb bombs by then, two or three to an aeroplane and when they were bombing Berlin they had those blockbusters that were absolutely enormous things.

The crew was five to an aeroplane. They looked pretty disreputable dressed in what looked like workman's overalls and they climbed into the aircraft in the middle. When they wanted to get out, they climbed out just underneath the nose, about half way between the nose and the propellers; the pilots sat up above this.'

At this stage of the war, navigational aids were primitive and the crew members were not always able to identify the target visually, so to get from point A to Point B they needed to rely on calculating their position over the intended target using mainly a chart, a clock and a compass.

John flew nineteen bombing missions, usually in a Whitley Mk V, registration T4165, against targets varying from the French and Belgian channel ports to railway marshalling yards and oil refinery plants in Germany, with two attacks over Berlin. These operations did not all go according to plan. On one occasion, having completed the bombing, the aeroplane had only one functioning engine by the time it crossed the Dutch coast on the return journey, keeping low in case it became necessary to ditch into the sea, he needed all his skills to bring the aeroplane home successfully.

John's logbook entry for 8th November 1940 records that he flew to RAF Honington, West Suffolk to await the start of what was supposed to be his 13th operational sortie. He was in the Whitley Mk. V that had been his regular aircraft since becoming an operational aircraft Captain on 18th October. His crew were Plt Off James, 2nd Pilot, Sgt Gibson, Navigator, Sgt Martin, Wireless Op/Air Gunner and Sgt MacMillian, Rear Gunner. He wrote 'Operation cancelled owing to damage to aircraft caused by enemy bombs, enemy aircraft destroyed on Aerodrome.' This was the second time within seven months that John was positioned very close to an exploding bomb.

Four Whitley bombers were awaiting take off on a raid to Italy when a 7/KG1 Junkers Ju 88A-5 (2186) aeroplane, believed at the time to be a Blenheim, circled the airfield at 18:00. It then returned at 18:18 and dropped four or five bombs along the length of the flare path. Initially one station gunner opened fire, followed by others, and the aircraft crashed near D Hangar at 18:20. The crew all bailed out but were killed and the aeroplane was destroyed. The gunner who first opened fire was put on a charge for opening fire without permission but was later awarded the Military Medal.

The following day John piloted the damaged Whitley to Dishforth for repair, taking with him only Sgt Gibson, the Navigator and Sgt Martin the Wireless Operator with him as crew, and an LAC Henderson (ground crew) as passenger.

John did not fly again until the 13th, when he was at the controls of the repaired T4165 for an air test, flying with all his normal crew. That night he flew his thirteenth Operational Sortie to Leuna.

On his 18th mission, on 19th December, there was an icing problem followed by a heavy barrage immediately after the bombs were dropped. Wireless transmitter and receiver trouble ensued and the flying instruments became unserviceable. All these problems were bad enough, but the icy conditions froze the pipes leading from the auxiliary and fuselage petrol tanks needed for long flights, leaving only the fuel in the wing tanks to supply the engines. It was a huge relief for everyone when he managed to land safely at base.

The main base for German attacks on the convoys bringing supplies from North America to Britain was the North Coast area of Brittany. The U-boat operations were directed from headquarters at Lorient. The RAF began to bomb the U-boat pens, so the Germans built reinforced concrete shelters; in spite of the RAF scoring a number of direct hits, their bombs could not break through the concrete that shielded the submarines, but there was a large amount of damage to the nearby towns.

On 28th December, after spending Christmas in England, John and his crew took the standby aeroplane P4950 on a raid against the submarine base at Lorient in Brittany. While flying over Bristol there was a problem with the cooling pipe affecting the starboard engine. There was a specific problem with the Whitleys; the starboard engine serviced all the hydraulics and the port engine serviced all the electrics. The landing gear could be handled manually but there was no alternative way of manoeuvering the flaps. John had to throttle back on the starboard engine, managing to maintain height at about 10,000 feet with more power on the port engine and with the starboard engine at about half throttle. The crew were keen to complete the operation and they continued to the target, which the crew spotted through a gap in the clouds; the bombs were released bang on time. As they left the target area, an anti-aircraft shell exploded just under the port wing tip and set the engine on fire. In John's own words:

'We began to lose height. I thought it over carefully; we were about 10,000 feet and about 100 miles from the French coast, and with luck we could get half way back across the channel before we had to ditch in the sea. Unfortunately, ten minutes later we were losing height much too quickly and my altimeter was showing about 1200 feet and I knew that the ground I was travelling over would be anything up to 7 or 800 feet.'

John called back to the crew that it was time to leave. Initially the crew were reluctant to jump over enemy territory, so a short argument ensued; but then John ordered them to jump for their lives, and all four left the aircraft, leaving John on his own with 1200 feet in hand. He was aware that there were hills in Brittany that were 1000 feet high. The second pilot had pushed his chair back, uncovering the escape hatch, which was positioned forward of the second pilot's seat. John undid his straps, dived straight through the hatch and pulled the ripcord as soon as he was clear. The next thing he remembered was landing in a muckheap in the corner of a churchyard. This had at least softened his landing, so he considered it lucky. The aircraft crashed in flames just two fields away.

Sgt AJ MacMillan, the rear gunner, landed from 1200 feet and went into hiding. He would later meet up with John in Nantes, having been helped by the same organisation. The two of them were in constant touch until his arrest in the middle of September. PO JET Louden, the second pilot, descended by parachute from a height of 1000 feet, twisted his ankle on landing, and was captured by a German patrol while his foot was being bandaged by a Frenchman. Sgt GW Wilmore, the Navigator, was captured on landing. Sgt LA Beckett, the Wireless Operator, landed safely from 600 feet and was given food and drink by a farmer, who later betrayed him. All three of them were flown to Germany on 29th December.

Somewhat bruised and shocked, John was surrounded within two or three minutes by three men; they bundled up his parachute and took him, hobbling on a damaged ankle, to a house nearby and there he was given a hot drink. Shortly after that a woman called Mme. Faubel arrived and indicated that there was a German patrol in the neighbourhood looking for people, so he was escorted back through the village, which was quite dark. John was told that there were people in the road, so he should use the fields and get away as quickly as possible from the scene. John had hurt his ankle when he landed, but considered himself to be very fortunate; when he investigated a bruise on his inner thigh, he found that a piece of shrapnel had hit a coin in his trouser pocket, which had probably saved his life. He carried this misshapen silver florin with him for the rest of the war.

These early days of his evasion were difficult in the extreme. He was still feeling the after effects of his awkward landing and the shock of the experience of dealing with an aeroplane on fire that was heading for a crash landing. He didn't speak French; he had learned a little French at school but didn't remember much that was of any use. John headed towards the coast to try and find a boat. Walking sometimes by day and sometimes by night, John walked through the fields in the cold rain. Finding a boat proved to be impossible. Eventually, John spoke to a fisherman who warned him that all boats leaving were checked by German patrols and that any of the smaller boats that went out past the rocks were smashed by the Germans when they returned. Life seemed pretty hard at that point as John considered his options. He decided to head for Spain, in spite of the long distance involved. To his horror, he found notices plastered up all over the place with a stark warning to anyone who was caught helping British or Allied airmen. The translated sign read:

'Notice: Every male individual who directly or indirectly helps crews of enemy airplanes dropped by parachute or by a forced landing, or helps their escape, or hides them in any possible way will be immediately shot.

Women guilty of the same will be immediately deported to concentration camps inside Germany.

Persons who capture crews constrained to land or of parachutists or who contribute by their attitude to their capture will receive a reward that could reach 10,000 francs. In some particular instances, this reward will be increased.'

In the pouring rain at around midnight on 31st December 1940 he found a barn to shelter in. He crawled up into the hayloft and slept, the cattle below providing a rudimentary form of central heating.

It was broad daylight when he woke. As he tried to sneak out of the barn he was accosted by people from the farm, who took him into the house and tried to find out who he was. He had been spotted the night before by Jean Le Goff, a young man of nineteen who worked at the farm. Jean had seen him on the road about one kilometre away from Bourg de Pléhédel, in the direction of Plouha.

The group of men did their best to kit John out with civilian clothing; he was taller than any of them, so it was quite difficult to make him look as though the clothes belonged to him. John saw some German lorries loaded with fragments of his aeroplane. The locals told him that the remainder of the burnt out wreck had been taken by neighbours for souvenirs.

He was then taken to the home of Francois Martin in a hamlet in Kereven; it was all very difficult. He looked odd to them as he was so dishevelled and was wearing his RAF uniform over his pyjamas, presumably having had to set off on the ill-fated operation at very short notice. The Bretons chose not to speak French, as they were very proud of their own language. This they combined with some French words into what was almost a kind of patois. John was interrogated by the men, who were seated around the table while the ladies stood around the wall. After a while, John's halting explanations, coupled with his uniform, seemed to satisfy them. Two of the ladies distributed steaming bowls of hot coffee, handing one to John first and then to each of the men. At this point the patron produced what John took to be a large bottle of water and handed it to him, indicating that he should cool his coffee. John was looking forward to his drink and poured a liberal amount of the liquid into his coffee. He was surprised to see that the other gentlemen each poured about a thimbleful into their coffee before handing the bottle on. When John drank the welcome beverage, he found out that what he'd assumed to be water was, in fact, almost pure alcohol. After the initial shock, he thoroughly enjoyed it and drained the bowl of coffee without spilling too much. The farmer then switched on the radio, John heard Big Ben strike twelve and a voice declaring 'ici Londres, General de Gaulle parlez…' This was midday on 1st January 1941. New Year's Day. General de Gaulle had previously instructed the French to stay indoors on that day as a sign of non-cooperation with the German occupiers; now the General was giving them words of encouragement.

A couple of days later, Sgt Andrew MacMillan was picked up and housed in Bourg de Plélo. He had approached the home of Mme. Joséphine Gicquel in Fros en Trégomeur. He was dressed in his uniform, and must have wandered around aimlessly in the countryside until he was exhausted. He said that he had found Germans everywhere and was extremely worried about being followed. He explained to Mme. Gicquel that his name was MacMillan and he told her about his grandmother who lived in Belfast where, by a happy coincidence, her niece taught French. He spent the night in Fros en Trégomeur and was introduced to Monsieur Lemoine, an English teacher at the Saint-Charles College in Saint-Brieuc, who lived locally.

MacMillan was then collected by Georges Le Bonniec, who took him into his care. He began by hiding him in Goudelin with Mme. Le Boulzec, and then a few days later he took him back to Lanvollon into the care of his neighbour Monsieur André Marchais, the postmaster. Marcel Hévin then took him to the Mahés' residence, but it was judged to be wiser to send him on to the Roncin ladies on the Rue de l'Emery. In order to avoid attracting the neighbours' attention, or suspicion from occasional visitors, the new arrival passed for a victim from le Havre who was so shaken by the bombings that he had become deaf and mentally deficient.

In the meantime, John was taken to see the local priest, Father Jean Baptiste le Geay, who spoke English and looked after John while he made arrangements for a safe house away from the area.

Mme. Le Roy was a tradeswoman in Lanvollon who had put Jean Baptiste le Geay in touch with some trustworthy people. André Marchais was the local postmaster, a decorated veteran of the First World War, who was a dedicated resistance worker. He was in charge of dealing with all the local identity cards and was thus able to provide John with what he needed with the help of Monsieur Quéromès who provided the official seal of Pléhédel's town hall. The other man who helped was the local garage owner Monsieur George Le Bonniec; on 2nd January he drove John and Jean Le Goff to the nearest bus station at Béncch du Pludual in order to get to Saint-Brieuc, a journey of some 30 kilometres. From there, the two of them set off by train for the difficult journey to Nantes: they had to change trains twice, in Rennes and Redon. John was instructed to pretend to be deaf and dumb, as he did not speak French. It all went smoothly, in spite of a number of controls at the stations and on the trains. Following the advice of Brother Legeay, Jean Le Goff and his companion walked straight to Mme. de Bondy's residence, where John was pleasantly surprised to find another airman. Jean Le Goff took the train back that same evening. There was no room for John to stay in the two roomed flat, but they made enough space for him to spend one night there.

The following morning he was collected by Marcel Hévin, the leader of a local resistance group that passed on information from Nantes and the North Coast facilities. Marcel worked as a designer at SNCF. One of the first acts of public resistance to German occupation had been a small public demonstration of secondary school students at the Arc de Triomphe on 11th November 1940, when they celebrated the Allied victory over Germany in the First World War. This had inspired Marcel Hévin to set up his group and he established contact with London before the end of the following month.

Marcel took John to meet Madame Delavigne who had been a nurse in the First World War. Her husband Adrien had been in the tank corps and had been injured; he had been awarded the Croix de Guerre. This award was created to recognize French and Allied soldiers who were cited for their service during World War I, similar to the Mentioned in Dispatches used by the British. Madame Delavigne received the Médaille de la Reine Élisabeth in recognition of her wartime work as a nurse.

At the start of the Second World War, Adrien and Joséphine Delavigne were looking forward to their eventual retirement and moving to their holiday house in Lesconil but that was not to be. The couple were determined to assist the Allied cause and at this stage of the war were making pamphlets on an old British Army typewriter stolen from the Germans. The main access to their house was a door between two shops leading to a courtyard at the back. It proved to be an ideal hiding place for John, as the front door could easily be observed simultaneously by two people from the same group who lived in the neighbouring houses, and in case of emergency, they were briefed to put a towel in the front window, then one could very easily escape via the exit on the side of the building.

John arrived there fairly early in the morning, to be told that he could not stay more than one night because Monsieur Delavigne was the Chief Executive of Lefèvre Utile, better known by the initials LU, a biscuit manufacturer who supplied the Germans and he had to have them in his house for meetings. John thought that even this was too dangerous for them, but they invited him to have a much needed bath and then sent him up to bed where he went into a deep sleep.

John's room was right at the top of the house. He heard later that his long sleep caused them some panic – to help him sleep well they had given him a nightcap of some eau de vie (a clear, colourless fruit brandy) and when he didn't reappear after many hours they looked at each other and tried to work out where they would put him if he had died. After due consideration they decided that they would somehow bring him down and put him into their home made air-raid shelter in the garden and fill it with earth. If anyone asked questions later, they would show them where he was. They were highly relieved when John eventually emerged and he stayed with them for a number of months, helping them with their work for the Resistance by collating and transmitting details of troop movements.

The Delavignes had no children, but their nephew Maurice Cybulski, a student at the Sorbonne, was a frequent visitor. The house was large and furnished with heavy drapes and furniture, much of it monogrammed. The couple prayed frequently at their prie-dieux in the main reception room and this is where Adrien conducted his business meetings with the Germans. Whenever these meetings were in progress, John would climb up to his hiding place in the roof rafters. Any vehicle coming to the house had to approach from the front and was visible for long enough for John to secrete himself away.

The typewriter lived in the kitchen and this is where all their resistance work took place. John was dressed to resemble a gardener whenever he was in the garden at the back of the house, just in case any pedestrian spotted him through the entrance between the shops leading from the road. In truth it was very difficult to find clothes for him, as the other two men were so much shorter than John.

Conversation was difficult. John did not speak French and Madame Delavigne did not speak English, but they became very fond of John and she soon became 'Tantine'. Adrien did not speak German; this put him at a disadvantage in his business meetings. However, John had studied German as his European language at school, so he had some useful knowledge. Tantine went out and bought a selection of dictionaries: English-Spanish, Spanish-French, Spanish-German, German-French. Then, at every mealtime, they made themselves reply in the required language. John had to work out what they were saying in French first and then translate from a dictionary into German, from there to Spanish, and finally into English. They then reversed the process; every meal took two to three hours. Tantine was careful to ensure that John learned French with a local dialect so that he could pass himself off as a workman when they finally found a route back for him.

During his time with the Delavignes, John was carefully schooled in unlearning much of what he had been taught about table etiquette. The British rules at the table were to be the downfall of many evading airmen; the way they placed knives and forks on their plate in any public place was an instant giveaway.

The following text is taken from *The Osterley Hints on Table Etiquette*:

'Put the knife and fork when not in use down on the plate, not as continentals do, hanging at the sides like the oars of a boat.

Disposal of knife and fork when not in use; at the conclusion of a meal, or of one of the courses, the knife and fork are placed side by side upon the plate somewhat to the right, sharp edge of knife inwards prongs of fork upwards.'

Shortly after John's arrival, two other airmen arrived. It proved difficult finding somewhere for them to stay. There was one place, a flat on the top floor of a house, the remainder of which was occupied by the Gestapo. The hosts did not tell the airmen this and they only found out when one of them had too much to drink and started to sing British and Irish songs. He was arrested within a few minutes, and John was told about it straight away by some neighbours who had dashed down the road to let him know. He immediately packed his belongings and was sheltered in another house nearby until it was safe for him to return.

Knowing the enormous risks involved in sheltering the airmen, Marcel Hévin worked very hard to find an escape route for them. No-one recommended that the evaders should attempt to travel without assistance; the paths to Spain across the unoccupied zone and the demarcation line were difficult to find. There were ongoing negotiations for help from the members of the Vandermotte-Clément group, but these came to nothing when the Germans arrested André Clément himself.

At the beginning of April, Marcel Hévin began to worry that he was about to be arrested. He became exceptionally careful and covered his tracks meticulously, telling his wife that there was nothing for the Germans to find. On 25th April, Mr. Klein from the Gestapo discovered nothing at all when he came to question and search him at Boulevard Gabriel Lauriol. Mme. Bouvier, a family friend from Alsace, went to the Gestapo's head-quarters at the Hôtel des Pyrénées to enquire about him and was told that Hévin had been arrested as a witness and middleman in some perceived crime. M. and Mme. Bouvier were part of the Hévin group, and he became Marcel Hévin's successor at the head of the organisation. The Germans had failed to find any evidence of Hévin's activities, but he was kept in prison and then transferred to the fort at Romainville with his friend Hubert Caldecott and the young Philippe Labrousse on 1st October 1941.

The Delavignes continued to help the Resistance through the Nantes branch of Côtes du Nord. They worked hard to get in touch with the British organisation, or that of General de Gaulle. In the middle of August, Andrew MacMillan was moved to the house of Madame Flavet and she by now had made contact with Claude Lamirault (codename Fitzroy) to arrange the onward journey for the two airmen. The recently formed Jade Fitzroy organisation was founded by the unlikely combination of Claude Lamirault, previously a member of the Camelots du Roi (literally 'street-hawkers of the king', the youth wing of Action Française, a French far-right political movement), and Pierre Hentic, a former member of the Young Communists. Claude was now actively planning the escape of the two airmen. On 21st September, the Flavet family were betrayed and they were arrested along with MacMillan. The news of these arrests reached John on 25th. Inevitably they would all be interrogated so it became necessary to move John immediately.

The Delavignes had no direct contact details for Claude Lamirault. However, they had a slight acquaintance with a 'so-called Pole', Stanislaus Ryps (actually a Hungarian Jew), in connection with passing letters into the Unoccupied zone. Ryps initially refused to help them.

He was an agent for a Polish network that collected military intelligence which was transmitted to England via the unoccupied zone. Stanislaus Ryps, alias Yves Le Poarec, stayed periodically with Mme. Mahé in Nantes for two days at a time and then left again with documents given to him by the Hévin-Barreau-Bouvier network. Mme. Mahé meticulously copied the reports onto onion-skin paper, a robust, translucent paper which was often used for carbon copies; it was chosen because it would remain in good shape in spite of being folded and squashed for a length of time. Ryps would conceal the documents inside his socks.

At this time he was staying with Mme. Pichon, a neighbour of Mme. Delavigne, and was becoming increasingly concerned about being followed. He now intended to get to England in order to undergo parachute training for future missions. He confided in Gilles Mahé that he did not want to use the route that he normally used in order to cross the demarcation line. The people from Nantes asked him whether he would like to take John Mott to the Spanish border instead. He accepted once a suitable financial arrangement had been agreed. On the night of 26th September, Ryps and John set off from 6 Boulevard Amiral Courbet on bicycles, John having been given Maurice Cybulski's cycle. The two of them travelled on the express train to Bordeaux then went to the house of a Pole called Selk living in St. Sulpice des Pommieres, by Sauveterre de Guyenne (Cirende). John began to lose faith in Ryps, but there was nothing for it but to continue the journey with him. On 3rd October, Ryps bought train tickets to Poitiers on the demarcation line. They travelled to the stop before Poitiers and ambled through the fields until they reckoned they were over the line. Ryps then went to the local Post Office and had a look at the map, deciding that they were clear of the German area. They then travelled on a series of buses and trains for short journeys until they reached the border area at Aix les Thermes, where Ryps left John while he ostensibly went to collect some more evaders. John stayed in the house of the local schoolmaster who was happy to help him. The plan was for John to catch the local train at 06:00 the following morning to meet up with the rest of the group. The obvious destination in Spain was Andorra. Sensing John's concerns, the schoolmaster persuaded him that it would be better to divert to Barcelona; John trusted his judgement. He was instructed to catch a train travelling in the opposite direction at 06:30 the following morning and look out for a lady dressed in a particular way. John was on the station platform at the appointed time but there was no sign of the lady who was going to help him. He boarded the train and watched out of the window; at the last minute, she dashed onto the platform and boarded the train a couple of carriages beyond John.

When the train stopped at a small station on the border at La Tour de Carol, John stayed in his seat waiting for his helper to leave; but by the time he gave her a head start and reached the exit it was closed. Fortunately, he found an alternative exit via the toilet entrance and followed her from a distance. After walking for some time in the direction of Puigcerda she tripped and her scarf fell off; without looking round she put her scarf back on her head. John by this time was quite close to her as he had maintained his walking pace. She suddenly pointed to a gate and said 'Patron'. John assumed that this meant go on, so he walked through the gate and carried on and up into the hills beyond. After a long and arduous journey, he came across a man and asked him in French whether he was in France or Spain. John didn't understand the reply. He had learned the words from the dictionary but didn't have any experience of the sound of spoken Spanish. John now assumed that he was in Spain, so he headed south by south-west through the hills, in the direction of Barcelona.

John never spoke of the difficulties he encountered, but he somehow managed to endure the journey. Tantine had packed his haversack with tinned food but John was too nervous to eat. He kept walking night and day using all his life skills to achieve his aim of reaching Barcelona. John was adept at navigating by the sun during the day and by the stars at night. He used a very old method of finding south at night; having found the pole star, he stood sideways on with his arms outstretched at shoulder height. With one fist pointing at the pole star he would turn his head and look along the other arm beyond his fist to spot a landmark that he could keep in his sight to aim at. He managed to find water that was pure enough to drink, and was spared the dreadful amoebic dysentery that affected a number of other evaders who crossed the Pyrénées to freedom over the next few years.

Eventually he was back at sea level after his arduous climb and descent. In the late afternoon he reached the outskirts of what he thought was probably Barcelona. There were too many people around so John backed away from the houses and hid in some trees until the next morning. He was still too anxious to open any of the tins and was living on nervous energy. The following morning, taking his courage in both hands, he walked down through the streets until he reached the centre of the city. He was trying very hard not to limp but it was taking all his concentration to put one foot in front of the other in a semblance of a normal gait.

He had no idea where the Consulate was; he had no address, so he walked round and round the larger streets looking at the brass plates on the walls until he became pretty close to despair. Then he saw another brass plate across the other side of a double carriageway, and in an upper window there was a Union Jack. The only problem was that there were two Spanish policemen positioned at the entrance. John straightened himself up and walked across the road, past the two policemen, then without hesitating to check the brass plate he went straight into the building and up the stairs to the second floor. Here he saw a notice showing that it was indeed the British Consulate, so he knocked on the door. John was greeted and questioned. For the next seventeen hours he was petrified, and kept imagining the sound of heavy feet coming up the stairs and in through the doors. He also found it impossible to speak English. He felt like he'd just stopped being an Englishman, and became incapable of saying what he wanted to say; exhaustion and lack of food had taken their toll.

John had schooled himself for nine long months not to think in English at all. He had concentrated on learning French, which Tantine and Adrien so carefully nurtured in him until it had become his primary mode of speech. He was ushered into an office and offered a seat; eventually he was asked if he would like a drink. When John requested a cup of tea, everyone relaxed and went out of their way to help him. He was instructed to write a report for the Air Ministry about all that had happened to him and he found it impossible. He had to write the whole report in French as best he could. He had conquered the spoken language but had no knowledge of the grammar, and no experience of writing in his adopted language. Eventually the report was complete, but John could not put his feet to the ground in their appalling state; they were just a mass of bleeding blisters. The diplomatic car was driven to the door and John was taken to the home of the chauffer, a couple of miles away. Here the chauffeur's wife looked after him and tended his feet until they healed, which took about two weeks.

John returned to the consulate for a couple of days before he commenced his journey. Initially delighted to be stepping into the embassy car, he was a bit put out when he was told to climb into the boot. He then found himself covered by some heavy sacks of potatoes and travelling in no small discomfort. It wasn't long, however, before he became grateful that this course of action had been taken. It turned out that even diplomatic cars were checked by the Spanish guards, and to John's horror they were stopped on the road to Madrid at the main checkpoint and the car was searched;

the guards opened the boot and started pushing bayonets through the potato sacks. John came to no harm and was greatly relieved to arrive safely at his destination. At the British Embassy, John completed a report on the electrical power system in Southern Brittany and gave it to the Air Attaché. Having helped with the resistance work carried out by the Delavignes, he had made a mental note of anything useful that he had observed on his journey. He met two or three other evading airmen and they stayed there, within the compound, until tickets had been obtained for them to travel by train from Madrid to La Linea on the border with Gibraltar where, after a little more difficulty, they were allowed to enter the colony on 14th November.

In Gibraltar there were a number of evading airmen, impatiently waiting for transport home. John spent his time working out ways of improving the transport arrangements to remove the bottleneck. Every aeroplane carried a dinghy that could accommodate eight passengers for use in the event of a ditching; John was determined that the amount of personal baggage allowed on board should be drastically reduced so that a second dinghy and more passengers could be transported. The airmen awaiting transport formed a close bond at this time, because they had all come through the horrors of their experiences. John teamed up with three others and spent many hours at the bridge table before he made his own arrangements to get home. In the years after the war, the trio he left behind took every opportunity to remind him that it had been a pretty poor show to break up 'The Bridge Foursome'.

Waiting for the next troopship was becoming tedious so, while chatting to F/L Hodgkinson, the Captain of Australian Sunderland Flying Boat W3986, they cooked up a plan whereby John could fly with him and his crew, as 'supernumerary crew' on their flight to Pembroke Dock. On 13th December they flew from Gibraltar to RAF Mount Batten in Plymouth Sound and on the 15th they flew on to Pembroke Dock.

John was interviewed by MI9 and AI1(k) department compiled an interrogation report on 16th December. He then obtained a travel warrant to his hometown of Wallington with orders to report to the Air Ministry immediately after Christmas. On a dark December evening, with the blackout in force, John knocked on the door of 48 Marchmont Road. Believing that his son was dead, Arthur was so shocked when he saw John standing there that he immediately closed the door; once he had gathered his thoughts, and possibly thinking of the frugal supplies in the pantry, he then opened the door and reputedly said 'Hello Arnold, will you be staying for Christmas?' Sending John to find his mother, Arthur went out into the dark, found his ladder, and climbed up to the roof so that he could hoist the Union Jack for the neighbours to see in the morning.

There is no explanation of why John's parents had not been informed from Gibraltar that John was alive and on his way home. Tantine had picked up the good news sometime in November when the agreed message came through on the radio; 'LOUIS ENVOI AMITIES'.

3

LYSANDER DOWN

John spent a few days at home over Christmas. His Uncle Walter pursued a very successful life in South Africa and he supplied a regular stream of food parcels to the family to help them to overcome the wartime shortages. They never wanted for butter or dried fruit, so a traditional Christmas cake had been baked. It would not have been long before Arnold's gingerbread appeared for afternoon tea. There was news of two new grandchildren but they were far away from Wallington. In John's absence, Pip's daughter Judith had been born in Australia. When Pip shipped out to Basra he sent his pregnant wife off to stay with Mott family relations. Minna travelled from India to Sydney for the duration. The news of the birth of the baby reached England long before Pip finally received some letters bringing him up to date. Mervyn's wife and daughter had travelled to her home in Ireland where their son Martin had been born at the end of November, and they had not yet made the return journey. Christmas in Wallington had looked as though it would be pretty bleak and lonely until that knock on the door.

John reported to London as instructed, and here he got a bit of a dressing down at the Air Ministry for arranging his own transport home. Eventually he was sent to MI9 for interrogation and was quick to voice his opinion that an aircraft like the Lysander could be used for pick up so that evaders wouldn't have to walk so far. His interrogator questioned him very closely as to where he had heard about this. After some lengthy discussions, it was established that John was completely unaware that Lysanders were already being used for this purpose. He was then passed on to IS9; this was the newly formed Intelligence School 9 established as the executive branch of MI9. Its job was to assist British and Commonwealth service personnel to evade capture when behind enemy lines and to assist prisoners of war to escape. IS9's most important work was to gather intelligence from and boost the morale of Allied POWs. John gave them all the information he could and he was then invited to join 138 Special Duties Squadron. It was explained that agents were to be dropped by parachute into Europe and picked up later by Lysander. Returning airmen being debriefed by MI9 were accommodated together, and it was here that Alex Nitelet and John struck up their enduring friendship.

At the beginning of 1941, six Whitley aircraft had been converted for dropping commandos behind enemy lines by parachute. To reduce drag, the turrets and armaments were removed. There was a large square hole rigged with static lines for the parachute drops, which took place much closer to the ground than on normal operations. Clambering on board was somewhat difficult; the men were loaded down with parachutes, weapons, grenades, and ammunition. A converted Whitley was grossly uncomfortable. The men sat on the metal floor, trying to avoid the ribs of the fuselage. The airplane was very cold, especially after the cover was removed from the jumping hole in the bottom of the fuselage. Many of the men climbed into sleeping bags or wrapped themselves in blankets for warmth. The aircraft interiors were noisy, smelly and cramped, with movement restricted to crawling on hands and knees.

On 10th February, Whitleys from 78 Squadron and No. 51 Squadron flying from Malta were used to drop paratroops over Southern Italy for Operation COLOSSUS, the first British airborne operation of the Second World War. Thirty eight men led by Major T Pritchard blew up a fresh water aqueduct near Calitri in Southern Italy. This supplied some two million people, including the ports of Bari and Brindisi and the naval base of Taranto.

Three of these Whitleys were transferred to 138 (Special Duties) Squadron when it was formed in August 1941, at Newmarket. By the time that John was posted to the squadron in January 1942, it had moved to Stradishall in Suffolk, with twelve Whitleys, three Halifaxes and three Lysanders. Here, on 24th January, John was at the controls of Z9129 for a thirty-minute local air test. Then, on the 28th, he was in a Tiger Moth with Wing Commander Fairly for a short flying test and local flying practice.

On that same night, Captain John Nesbitt-Dufort, known as 'Whippy', was at the controls of a Lysander that took off at 20:00 heading for Le Fay, a former military airfield seven kilometres southeast of Issoudun, close to the village of Ségry. In France the agent André Simon was leading the reception committee for the operation; he was the son of the founder of the Food and Wine Society and bore the same name. André stowed the luggage himself then climbed back down the ladder. The two passengers that were picked up were Maurice Duclos, aka 'Saint-Jacques' and Lieutenant Mitchell aka 'Roger'. Maurice Duclos had founded the first Free French Intelligence network. He was a pre-war convicted Cagoulard (a right wing extremist organization). Lieutenant Mitchell was a French gunner officer whose family was bilingual; initially, General de Gaulle had sent him into France in the guise of an Englishman to liaise with the Poles. His current task was to ensure the safe return of Maurice Duclos to England. After take-off, the weather deteriorated to such a degree that the Lysander eventually had to land in a field back in France just eighteen kilometres from Issoudun. Having slipped on the frosty grass, the Lysander ended up nose down in a ditch where all attempts to destroy it failed. However, the three men evaded capture; they were sheltered by the Resistance and were successfully picked up in March. The local resistance members towed the abandoned Lysander onto a level crossing when a train was due and it was completely destroyed.

Squadron Leader John Nesbitt-Dufort had joined Special Duties the previous May, and from the beginning had been involved with training agents in how to select suitable fields and lay out skeleton flare paths for the Lysanders. One of his early trainees was Claude Limerault, aka 'Fitzroy', whose Jade Fitzroy intelligence network was controlled by Commander Biffy Dunderdale at MI6. From the information now available it seems likely that Mme. Flavet's inability to make contact with Claude Limerault to organise John Mott's journey back from Nantes was owing to the fact that Claude was undergoing training in the fields of Cambridgeshire with John Nesbitt-Dufort at the time when John Mott needed to be moved so urgently.

John Mott commenced his flying training on Lysanders in March. By the time he completed his training he had transferred to the newly formed No. 161 Squadron now based at Tempsford, alongside the already existing No. 138 Squadron. The secrecy surrounding the airfield at Tempsford was such that whenever night flights were taking place, all the telephone boxes in the area were chained and padlocked to prevent information leaks. The local baker was allowed to deliver bread to inside the perimeter but all other supplies had to be left at the gate. The Lysanders were specifically used to transport Allied agents into and out of France by night. In order to reduce fuel consumption, the Lysanders and their crews deployed to Tangmere for their operations. These took place from one week before until one week after the full moon.

The Lysander MkIII was flown by moonlight, with only a map and compass for the pilot to navigate to a field where three hand held torches indicated the landing strip. The Lysander had entered service before the war to be used for spotting and reconnaissance. Now modified, it came into its own with the moon squadrons. Weighing just over two tons and with a long wingspan, it could land and commence turnaround within 150 yards if necessary. Significantly, it could fly under the enemy radar and fly as slowly as 55mph without stalling. The strong undercarriage was formed by an alloy beam in the shape of an inverted V, and this enabled the 'Lizzie' to cope well when landing in rough fields. The high wings gave the pilot a good view downward on both sides. All non-essential equipment was stripped out to increase the range as much as possible. Due to the addition of a torpedo-shaped 150 gallon long range fuel tank underneath the fuselage, the round trip could be as much as 1,150 miles. The flaps were controlled automatically by special slats, allowing for a very steep final approach to landing. The aircraft was painted black and a fixed ladder was added on the port fuselage. The top rungs of the ladder were painted yellow so that the agents could easily board and exit the aircraft. The standard procedure was that agents arriving from England passed down their luggage and then stowed any inbound luggage under the rear-facing bench seat before climbing down the ladder. The waiting passengers then boarded the Lysander and closed the rear cockpit, so ideally take off could be just three or four minutes after landing.

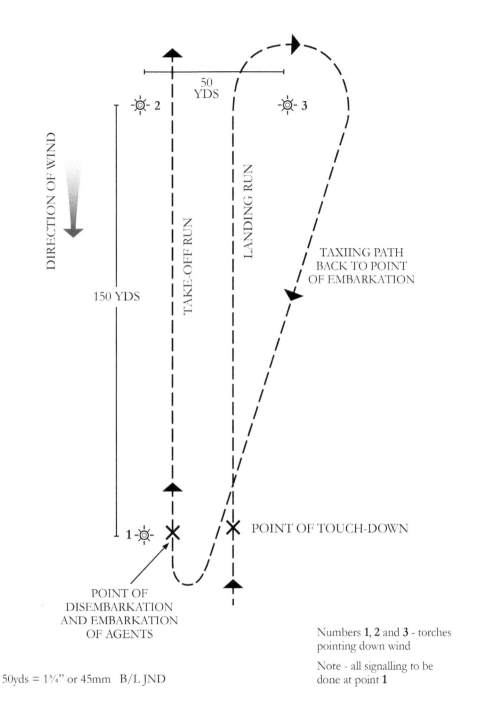

LANDING APPROACH DIAGRAM FOR LYSANDER PILOTS.

The pilots were an elite group whose skills were finely honed. Each of them had been invited to join the squadron because of their particular aptitudes and backgrounds. In John's case, many aspects of his life thus far led to his suitability for this specific role. Picking up the threads of his own life after a year away from all contact was made easier by the fact that time off was much more generous than for any other pilots in Bomber Command. It had been very difficult for the Mott family to cope with the fact that he had been presumed dead, but he had also left his pre-war fiancée, Whynifred Bignall, coping with the situation. She worked in London and John was able to spend time with her and renew their relationship when he was off duty. During the weeks spent in Tempsford between the moon periods, the group of pilots whiled away the hours when they were off duty playing parlour games or card games including bridge. A Victorian parlour game called 'Moriarty', after the character in the Sherlock Holmes stories, created a lot of noise and confusion, while the men placed bets on the outcome. Two men were blindfolded and lay face down on the floor. They kept contact with each other by clasping their left hands. Each of them held a rolled up newspaper in their free hand and they attempted to score by hitting the other man around the head with the newspaper. They played in turn by one of them calling out 'are you there, Moriarty?' The opponent called 'yes' and moved his head out of the way as quickly as possible. This harmless activity caused great hilarity.

John had almost completed a month on Lysanders when he was called on to take the controls of a Whitley for one last time. On 30th April he spent half an hour completing a night flying test on Z6940. The procedure at Tempsford was highly organized, and in the case of SIS Operations the passengers were kept away from the crew until the flight. The passengers were delivered to Gibraltar Farm, which was the nerve centre of the airfield. They were taken to a barn, which looked like an old farm building from the outside. However, the interior was highly organised and all the final preparations took place without any contact with the crew. Once the Whitley was ready for take-off, any passengers were handed over to the despatcher, who would be their only contact for the duration of the flight.

Thus, John may never have known that Operation WHITSUN was delivering Claude Limerault back to France to pick up the pieces of his network, which had suffered due to a betrayal while he was in England. He had been brought to England with his wife in a 161 Lysander on 1st April. He had requested a blind drop to return to his organisation and this had been agreed. John had recently been promoted from

Flight Sergeant to Pilot Officer and was at the controls of the Whitley. The procedure was that the crew boarded their aircraft and started up the engines. The passengers were then brought to the aircraft where they were received by the despatcher. They would then remain with him at the rear of the aircraft and the only other person who might see them would have been the engineer, who occasionally had to carry out checks throughout the aircraft. On this flight take off was at 00:15 and the aircraft reached Tangmere at 2,500 feet then crossed the French coast at 01:58 near Cabourg. It was now travelling at 7,000 feet and kept north of Evreaux and Dreux. The drop zone was near Saint-Hubert, 8.6 kilometres Northeast of Rambouillet (48° 43' N – 01° 51' E). At 03:00 assisted by the despatcher Sgt Wooly of 138 squadron, the agent was successfully dropped from 1,500 feet and he signalled to acknowledge his safe landing. Somehow the return past Evreaux and Dreux was slightly off course and the Whitley flew over German airfields near each of the towns. They experienced light flak when they were caught in searchlights from both fields, the rear gunner F/O Stephen attempted to destroy the searchlights. The aircraft was at 7,000 feet over Cabourg en route for Tempsford but the weather closed in and they were diverted to Boscombe Down arriving 5.25 hours after take-off.

PAUL MARITZ, WIKIMEDIA COMMONS

Living at close quarters was not always easy and while based at Tangmere it was necessary for the men to share the small bedrooms. John's years in boarding school meant that he had no problem on this front. In his book *We Landed by Moonlight* Hugh Verity writes that he found it difficult to share a bedroom with Guy Lockhart who preferred to sleep with the window closed. On the other hand I found it interesting to listen to Len Ratcliffe when he gave a talk at Tempsford in 2015, even after all these years he remembered how difficult he found it to share a bedroom with Hugh Verity.

The agents were known as 'Joes', whether male or female. In the case of the Lysander passengers, the pilots were responsible for briefing them. Usually they shared a meal in the cottage at Tangmere before the flight. The passengers needed to know how to open and close the rear cockpit and what to do in the case of an emergency in flight. The two cockpits were back-to-back and the intercom was to remain silent unless voice communication became essential. On arrival at the destination, the pilot kept his attention on landing and taking off as speedily as humanly possible so his passengers had to cope with the help of the reception committee on the ground.

Since his return to England, Alex Nitelet had completed his training and Jimmy Langley of MI9 was anxious to return him to France as the new wireless operator for the PAT Line. Initially the plan was for him to travel on Operation CHRISTMAS. André Simon had been in France since the beginning of May, facilitating the exfiltration of Édouard Delaldier aka 'Christmas', the ex-Prime Minister of France. In the end, Christmas was not willing to accept the risks involved and found a number of reasons for delaying the operation so the mission was postponed until at least the moon period at the end of June. However, there was an SIS pickup operation scheduled for 28th May, to collect members of the Jade-Fitzroy network. Claude's wife Denise was the niece of Emile and Gilberte Champion who were due to be brought to England with their son. Alex had recovered from the operation to remove his useless eye but he had also suffered from other injuries when his Spitfire was shot down and a parachute jump was not appropriate. In fact the after effects of his injuries troubled him for the rest of his life and they were ultimately the cause of his death. No longer fit to fly, he was now anxious to get back to the war and to help the members of the Escape Line who had organised his evasion.

John and Guy Lockhart spent the day of 28th May preparing for their flights that night. In John's case, the disused airfield at Le Fay had been successfully used before, so there was plenty of information to hand, as well as original photographs taken by reconnaissance aircraft. The accepted method of preparation was to cut the relevant strip out of a map including about 50 miles either side of the intended landing site; the strip was then folded like a concertina so that the pilot could hold it in one hand for reference whilst flying the aircraft with the other hand. There was a fixed map case on the port side of the cockpit, but a map of this size could be pushed into the top of a flying boot. Information including the latest weather and the beacon signals for the return leg were later written onto gen cards, which were then taped onto the map. It is difficult to ascertain precisely which escape aids were supplied to the pilots by the end of May 1942 as these were constantly being updated but it seems certain that John would have learned from his previous experience. His feet never quite recovered from the traumatic abuse they suffered as he crossed the Pyrénées, so a pair of his own shoes must have featured in his personal equipment. During operations, most of the Special Duties pilots wore a selection of civilian clothing underneath their flying suits. It was also a requirement that the bedrooms in the cottage were left as though they were not returning to the station, so all personal belongings were packed up. The packed luggage often included personal letters to be sent on if they were posted missing.

Guy Lockhart took off from Tangmere on SOE Operation GEAN in Lysander V9597 at 23:25. He was carrying one passenger and 150lbs of baggage and intended to fly to a landing field north of Châteauroux, 2 kms east of Les Vignots. Although the weather was fine across the Channel, it deteriorated as he approached his target area. He received no return signal from either the landing field or the two alternate fields. After circling for an hour, he was forced to abandon the mission and return to Tangmere, landing at 05:20.

Guy had been due to pick up André Simon who had been taken into France on 5th May. André had diverted his attention from the postponed Operation CHRISTMAS to spend time visiting agents to gain useful knowledge of the conditions around France. He requested a pick-up at the end of the month so that he could complete his report and return in time to collect Edouard Delaldier. Initially André's pick-up was scheduled for 26th May, but this was not possible so he checked into a hotel in Châteauroux. That night was the eve of a visit of Marshall Petain, the Prime Minister of Vichy France, to the town so the Special Police visited all the local hotels. All luggage and identity cards were examined then the Police Inspectors left. André had dual citizenship and was travelling on his own papers. However the inspectors reported the contents of Simon's luggage to their superior who insisted on questioning André himself. It was difficult to explain away four torches, 72,000 francs and the plans of a house in Juan les Pins. After four hours it became obvious that André's recent activities would be checked out so, to protect his recent contacts, he staged a breakdown and admitted that he had come from England.

He now spun a feasible, fictitious story and this was sent to Vichy at which point the dossier was handed to the military authorities. This resulted in questioning by a Gestapo agent posing as a French policeman. Fortunately the local French policemen had warned André that the man was an imposter. After about ten days in the civil prison in Châteauroux two officers came to tell him that he would be moved to the military prison in Perigueux. They questioned him about his feelings for France and his experiences during the war. After a while they asked him who had been his Chef de Bataillon during his French military service in 1928. He could not remember the name but they told him that le Général Roux remembered him. This was because André had been brought up in England and educated at Stoneyhurst so when he commenced his military training his French was hesitant and this had made him conspicuous. It was also the case that Colonel Fagalde had served as Military attaché in London and had originally introduced André and his Father to his Chef de Bataillon. The conversations developed into a request for André to return to England and instigate communication between the French Army and the British Army so that the French Army could go back into action in the event of the British Army landing on French soil. This was to be a military operation kept in the strictest secrecy and the de Gaulle organisation was to be kept out of the plans. The two officers warned André Simon that it would probably take two months before his liberation could be arranged in a manner to satisfy the Gestapo. However, he was allowed out on bail on 9th July; this was obviously due to the suppression of evidence that would have been prejudicial to his case. André travelled to Lyon prior to leaving the country; here he had a last interview with the two officers and gave his parole that he would return to France to give them an answer, whatever happened.

In the conclusion of the report he submitted on his return, André commented on the lucky chance that General Roux had remembered him. Once he had been handed over to the military authorities, the police had no further interest in his dossier. The military provided him with authentic papers in his real name. He ended the report by stating his view that he should return to France to contact these two officers as soon as possible, taking with him an agreement, in principle, that the liaison was of interest to GHQ.

It goes without saying that André Simon had been in no position to make contact and cancel his pickup on 28th May. Likewise, he was unable to flag the fact that Marshall Petain was visiting the area and there was a flurry of military activity. The Jade-Fitzroy team were attempting to prepare the landing site for Operation TENTATIVE. The Germans always put telegraph poles across any disused airfields but when Claude and his team went to move the telegraph poles from the Le Fay airfield, the Germans were holding manoeuvres on the field. The troops had not moved away until late afternoon, which made it impossible for Claude and his team to remove the posts. By the time the troops had moved away, it was too late to contact London so they hastily sought out a suitable field nearby. John only made sense of the sequence of decisions and events of that night decades later, when a member of the reception committee visited England, on a trip hosted by the Royal Air Forces Escaping Society.

When John took off from Tangmere, he found himself in thick cloud almost immediately. He had no sight of land with the exception of two small glimpses, which confirmed that he was on course. When he reached his estimated time of arrival, he dropped down through the cloud and immediately saw a torch signalling the agreed Morse code letter. He flashed back the return signal and flew across the field waiting for the landing strip to be highlighted. There were three torches, two a hundred yards apart with the third fifty yards to the right. Coming in to land John became concerned that the first landing light was very close to some tall trees. He felt secure in the knowledge that he had about half an aerodrome to land in so he aimed to touch down about half way along the landing path. As he landed he put the brakes on, intending to turn at a right angle as quickly as possible towards the third light; to his horror, there was a bump and the Lysander skidded straight forward and started to tip up. Then it came to a halt and when John got out to look he found that the plane was bogged down in mud. The farmer had ploughed the far end of the field earlier in the day, so the start of the landing strip had been sighted close to the other edge of the field.

The planned landing would have worked, if the agents on the ground had been able to convey to John that he needed to come in tight over the trees. Some of the reception committee rushed up to the Lysander and they all started to push and pull to get it out but with no luck. After three or four minutes, John noticed some lights in the distance and asked what was going on. The agent said that it was probably the army so there was no time to lose. John broke the IFF radio; this was used to identify Allied aircraft from those of the Axis powers, (Friend or Foe). In spite of his best efforts, he could not fire the aircraft so he had to leave it where it had stopped for the reception team to dispose of it. The Lysander was later removed by the Germans and exhibited in their museum of captured enemy equipment at Nanterre, near Paris, until they destroyed the museum during their retreat, in the summer of 1944.

In the meantime, Claude had disappeared into the night with Alex Nitelet and his bulky radio equipment. The second-in-command, Pierre Hentic, did his best to get John safely away. He gave John his own false papers and instructed him to cross two fields to the road on the other side, and then to follow it for about a quarter of a mile and look for a bicycle propped up against the wall of a post office. The demarcation line was about fifteen miles to the south along the road. John headed off but was then stopped by a gendarme on a bicycle who queried what he was doing out and about after the curfew time. He took John to the Police house and put him in a cell at the back of the house. John settled down in the rather flea-ridden cubby hole but he was pretty upset at having to face trying to escape rather than evade this time round. With all that had happened to him, he just could not get to sleep. Sometime in the small hours, he was rooting around and found that the door was not securely locked. He wasted no time in setting off to look for the promised bicycle. He found it easily, then hid in a ditch until dawn, when he set off quite merrily.

His luck ran out when he had a puncture and found that the bicycle had a pump but no repair kit. Sitting by the side of the road, he struggled to get the tyre off and decided to tie a knot in the inner tube. Before he could complete the task, a little Fiat Topolino 500 came along and stopped beside him. This small car (whose name translates as 'little mouse') was barely big enough for one person, but it contained two enormous policemen who offered their help. John thanked them but said that he was all but finished now. They asked to see John's bicycle permit and he explained that he had left it behind, at which point he was asked for his papers. Pierre Hentic had given John his own false papers when he sent him on his way. John was questioned and explained that he was a charcoal burner from Brittany. When the gendarmes asked to see his hands, they bore no resemblance to the hands of a charcoal burner so the game was up.

John was then taken to Châteauroux where the Commandant of the barracks was very pro-German and anti-British. It was unfortunate that the RAF chose that same night to do a leaflet drop in the area; the Commandant was quite certain that John had called the RAF on a secret radio. Fortunately no connection was made between John and Pierre

Hentic who had been arrested near the landing site without papers and arrived at the same prison. Pierre Hentic was put into the same cell as André Simon. The intervention of the military visitors in the case of André Simon might well have had something to do with the fact that Pierre Hentic was somehow able to escape from this prison and carry on with his resistance work.

John was unaware of the two other captives and he was later sent to the prison in the nearby town of La Châtre where he was locked up in solitary confinement and questioned for a number of days. The cruelty he endured was something that he was never willing to discuss, but some indication was given when he spoke of his next journey during a talk to the University Air Squadron decades after the war. Eventually, John was sent to a POW camp near Nice where he became a POW, rather than a civilian prisoner. The journey was very uncomfortable; John's escort strapped one of his hands up high to the luggage rack and the other hand was strapped low down to the support for the seat. He was given neither food nor drink. This train journey to Bordeaux took a full half-day. On arrival John was handed over to a local police sergeant who told him that he would take John down to the police headquarters where he would be registered and then given some lunch before continuing the journey. This policeman saw the state that John was in and then showed him a real kindness that probably prevented a catastrophic incident. John was asked to give his parole that he would not try to escape, and the policeman took him home to share lunch with him and his wife before returning to the railway station. When John went to visit Mme. Delavigne on her return from concentration camp, they worked out that on that particular day at lunchtime she was being interrogated by the Gestapo at the Bordeaux police headquarters where he had been heading. From information revealed by Ryps she was continually questioned about John Mott, who Ryps said she had sheltered for months on end. By disobeying his orders the unknown policeman had prevented the certainty of Arnold John Mott being identified in connection with Ryps and Tantine. Without knowing any of this, John enjoyed the best meal he had eaten since leaving Tangmere and then he and the friendly policeman got onto a train and continued the journey to Nice. Here John was put into a police car and taken to the Fort de la Revère.

Back in Tangmere, it must have been with a heavy heart that, on 29th May, Guy Lockhart picked up John's log book, completed the details of his flight the night before, and then signed the entry that showed John as 'Missing'. On 10th June, there was a communication from the Air Ministry Communications Section to

Commandant de Ryckman de Bets at the Belgian Embassy in Eaton Square, attached to copies of telegrams sent on 29th May, at 10:00. The first of these stated that Lysander 111a V9595 of 161 Squadron and Pilot Arnold John Mott 120214 were missing, kin informed; the second, that PO A.E.J.G. Nitelet 87699 (Navigator) was also missing, kin not informed.

4

TANTINE'S WAR

Speaking to a group of schoolchildren in 1996, John Mott began his talk by quoting from a sermon delivered in Brussels by the Chaplain to The Royal Air Force Escaping Society at a commemoration of the Comet Line (in French: Réseau Comète) on Sunday 24th October 1993. Reverend Bruce Lang has kindly permitted me to include some of his words here:

'As I read stories of Comète and Escapers, as I talk to people year by year, I often wonder at how ordinary they are. I don't mean ordinary in any critical sense, I am thinking of the many folk who came from ordinary situations and met an extraordinary need with extraordinary courage and wit. A nurse, a teacher, a gardener, an interpreter for the Germans, a Post Office engineer, a masseur; I could go on for a long time. Indeed, sometimes it was the very ordinariness which fooled the Germans.

It was this ordinariness that was involved in the creation of the lovely drink Kir, named after Canon Kir, who sheltered many thousands of French resistance fighters and evaders. Kir is ordinary white wine…. so ordinary in fact, that it is known apparently as rince cochon (pigswill). I intend no insult by taking the idea of ordinariness that far; but the white wine has cassis added, blackcurrant liqueur, to make it superb. It is sharp and refreshing, yet it is basically very ordinary then becomes something very special.

So many of you, by your experiences under occupation, by your upbringing of integrity, by your longings for a free Europe, by your own determination, were indeed being marked so that it became impossible to avoid being involved in Comète and other resistance work. Once that character is formed and you have been through the experiences, there is a certain inevitability about the resulting actions. What kinds of characters are being formed in Belgium/Britain today? What kind of experience do we offer our young people to mould their minds?

I wonder sometimes, as I teach; though I suspect that given similar circumstances, we should see strength and integrity suddenly being built in those characters. But, there is another parallel; again I do not make a generalisation. I speak to so many helpers who have real faith in God, a far higher proportion than I find generally. Is it their Faith that moulded their characters in the ways that led them into Resistance work? Is it their experiences and commitment to helping aircrew that caused them to search for a deeper meaning in life? Tell me if you know.'

Joséphine Delavigne (known to all the family as Tantine), and her husband Adrien would no doubt have described themselves as ordinary Bretons who had rebuilt their lives after their exemplary nursing and military service during the First World War. They each received a number of decorations for their service.[1] Adrien was a senior executive at Lefèvre-Utile and a patriotic Breton who was Vice President of an organisation involved with the revival of the old Celtic culture and language. They were both determined to help to overthrow the occupiers and worked hard producing pamphlets on an old British Army typewriter stolen from the Germans. The work was for a group headed by Marcel Hévin. Shortly after New Year's Day 1941, he asked them to look after a British airman; on 6th January he arrived at their house with Arnold John Mott, whose aircraft had come down in flames some days before.

It was not long before John had become like family to them and they did everything possible to prepare him for his journey back to England while actively trying to facilitate it. Marcel Hévin was arrested and they had no other link to anyone who could

---

1 On Tantine's death, John gave most of the medals and citations to the Church in Lesconil, in Brittany. This was where Tantine attended Mass near to the house where she lived out her old age. There is a window in the Church dedicated to the two of them.

help; they tried in vain to get in touch with the British organisation or that of General de Gaulle. However, Mme. Flavet made contact with the Jade-Fitzroy organisation at the beginning of August, and in mid August Tantine became involved with moving Andrew MacMillan from the home of M. Der Louise Ponsot in the Avenue de Grilland to stay with Mme. Flavet. Claude Lamirault (Fitzroy) was actively working to find a route home for the two airmen but unfortunately Mme. Flavet and her daughter were denounced on 21ˢᵗ September. Andrew MacMillan was arrested at their residence and spent the rest of the war as a POW. Mme. Flavet and her daughter were deported and only her daughter survived.

In the meantime Marcel Hévin was still in prison without any trial, as the authorities could not find any evidence of his activities. Life in Nantes changed dramatically on 20ᵗʰ October 1941, with the assassination of Lieutenant Colonel Karl Hotz, the Feldkommandant (German military governor) of Nantes. Hitler initially ordered the immediate execution of fifty suitable hostages; Marcel Hévin was one of the forty eight hostages who were shot in retaliation for the death of Hotz.

'Ici Londres. Voici quelques messages personnels' was the introduction that the BBC European Service used to broadcast messages after the evening news bulletins. Following the opening bars of Beethoven's Fifth Symphony, which represented the Morse code letter V for 'Victory', the requisite phrases were broadcast one after another. These only made sense to their intended target. The broadcast messages helped the clandestine wireless operators to limit their transmissions to the bare minimum while the enemy detector vans sought them out. Many types of messages were conveyed in this way between the Secret Services and the resistance, including notification of the successful conclusion of a 'home run' by an evader.

In the middle of November, when John reached Gibraltar, the Delavigne family were relieved to hear the BBC broadcast the agreed message 'LOUIS ENVOIE AMITIES' (Louis sends his regards).

The Delavigne couple continued their work gathering knowledge and passing it on to the Libération Nord until 5ᵗʰ March 1942 when, at one o'clock in the morning, they were arrested by the Gestapo. Adrien was taken to the Lafayette prison, a civilian prison in Nantes, and Tantine was taken to the Rue des Rochettes, a German military prison. On 9ᵗʰ March they were both moved to Bordeaux and incarcerated at the Fort du Hâ; this was a grim medieval fort that the Nazis were using as a political prison to lock up opponents and resisters. In the meantime, the Paris Gestapo arrested Maurice Cybulski, who was a student at the Sorbonne, and after three weeks at the Cherche-Midi prison, he was also taken to the Fort du Hâ.

Tantine was interrogated three times at great length. She knew that Ryps had a nervous disposition and was unlikely to withstand the interrogation techniques that would have been used on him; she soon realised that Ryps had betrayed all his contacts and greatly compromised her. She decided to deny everything, in spite of his testimony. She was confronted with him in the presence of the German staff of the prison and he repeated a number of times that he knew her but she just said that it might be possible that the gentleman knew of her in Nantes and she maintained that she did not know him.

In her report after the war, Tantine did not give details of her treatment during these interrogations. However, at some time when she was speaking to John she told him some further details of her treatment; she was 'helped to remember' the people she denied knowledge of by being held barefoot on an electric stove, with the result that she was unable to walk for some time after her release.

Ryps had specifically implicated only Tantine; her beloved nephew Maurice was released on 22nd June and her husband on the following day. Maurice had been taken ill while he was held in the severe conditions at the prison and, on his return to Paris, his condition deteriorated until he was admitted as an emergency case to Leemes. He died later in the Sanitorium of Saint-Martin-du-Tertre in Seine-et-Oise.

On 27th July, the German military tribunal in Paris held a special council in Bordeaux in order to judge Ryps and the people who were compromised by his confessions; this included M. Selk and Tantine. During the course of the six sittings of the council, Tantine was helped by a lawyer from Berlin and maintained that she did not know Ryps; he was found guilty and executed in July at the Fort du Hâ. The council members decided that Tantine was not of sound mind and acquitted her on 3rd August; she was liberated on the 28th.

This dreadful experience did not deter Tantine and Adrien from continuing their efforts to keep up the flow of information. Alongside this work, it was not long before they became involved with assisting other airmen.

On 28th June 1943, Monsieur Ferdinand Guimard from Ingrandes (Maine et Loire) called at the house. He was a student from the Locquidy College on Boulevard Michelet in Nantes and a friend of their nephew Maurice Cybulski; he was looking for a safe place for two airmen. On 19th June, a group of about thirty young people had been enjoying a secret dance at the Hotel de la Belle Etoile, hosted by Henry and Melanie Catrou. They danced the night away until, at the first light of dawn, someone called them outside to see an aeroplane that was on fire and heading for the ground. It was an RAF Lancaster belonging to Squadron 115 on its way back from a mine laying mission in the waters off La Rochelle. It broke up on crashing at the end of Ingrandes Bridge, in the corner of Mesnil en Vallée, and the debris was spread over a wide area. The youngsters started to look around for the members of the crew but the Gestapo arrived immediately, so they dispersed to their homes as quickly and quietly as they could. The following day some of them came across a young man who had been given ill-fitting civilian clothes by some locals. He had striking curly blond hair and did not speak any French but had a card with useful French phrases and a wad of French banknotes. He tried to make it clear that he wanted to head for Spain. Unfortunately, he looked far too conspicuous and he needed medical attention because he had damaged one of his ankles when he landed by parachute. Louis Ferdinand took nineteen-year-old Frank Trott to a safe place by horse and wagon, and those who had found him now sought the help of the local doctor. Dr. Doudeuil was brought to see Frank; he diagnosed a sprain and gave him an injection to relieve the pain. By the following day there was a definite improvement.

On Monday the news came out that Peter Brown, the pilot of the aeroplane, had drowned in the river Loire and that his funeral would take place in the local cemetery. On Tuesday they heard that another member of the crew was sheltering at a farm in Montjean. Louis Ferdinand hitched his horse to the wagon and went to collect Allan Sheppard who was very happy to meet up with Frank. Peter Brown was buried on the Wednesday and the group of friends promised that he would never be forgotten.

Louis Ferdinand arranged to accompany Ferdinand Guimard and the two airmen to Nantes to look for help. Dr. Doudeuil agreed to provide petrol for the car, as he had priority for supplies so that he could travel to the homes of his sick patients. The Germans had intensified their search for the remaining members of the crew, having rounded up the rest, so Ferdinand was very anxious to move Trott and Sheppard as soon as possible. On a Saturday morning, Alphonse Lechat, who was the mechanic at the Riottière garage, took them to Nantes in his old Citroën, which had not been used for a while due to the lack of available petrol. There were very few cars on the road and it was not long before the car showed symptoms of its lack of use; it broke down a short distance from a parked truck full of German soldiers. Allan got out of the car to help but was quickly persuaded to get back in due to his strange appearance in trousers that were barely below his calf. Alphonse managed to get the car going again and they reached Nantes without any further incidents.

For their part, Tantine and Adrien did everything they could to find these airmen a safe place. They tried every way they could think of to get in touch with the Marie-Claire network in Poitiers but this presented many difficulties.[2] Eventually, the vital connection was made. This involved Tantine taking a trip to Poitiers to contact the Marie-Odile escape line. Tantine visited Mme. Blanc and made contact with the group by using the password 'De la part du Dauphin', which had been given to her by André Coindeau, the head of the Alliance network for the Nantes area and Brittany. On 13th July, Frank Trott and Alan Sheppard were on their way home.

At the same time, the Delavignes were involved in looking after an American airman, Lieutenant Ralph D. McKee, who had bailed out of his aircraft on 4th July 1943 in the neighbourhood of St. Philbert de Grand Lieu and had been looked after by Mme. Cuilbaud at Le Hairion in St. Philbert. He was now one of a group of evaders who were to be escorted through France and on to Spain. They were moved individually to other safe houses while final arrangements were being made for their journey, to reduce the amount of activity around the house where all the planning was taking place.

Tantine returned from her trip to find that Ralph had been collected and was on his way to freedom. His group made the hazardous journey to the border and across the mountains into Spain, only to be stopped without papers by two armed Spaniards who belonged to the Guardia Civile. They were then thrown into gaol to wait for someone in authority to be contacted. Ralph developed amoebic dysentery from drinking the mountain water and he became very ill. Herded onto an old bus, the prisoners were taken to Pamplona and locked in a cell with only straw mattresses, a washbasin and a makeshift toilet in one corner. There followed a dreadful week until an American official arrived at the gaol to interview the Americans. Eventually the group of prisoners were moved to Alahama where they were helped by Lieutenant John Dunbar, a

---

2 Gertrude Mary Lindell was an English VAD nurse in WW1, highly decorated for her wartime work. She married a Frenchman and became Comtesse de Milleville. Codenamed Marie-Claire, she became active in the Resistance in 1940 and in 1942, setting up an escape line of the same name that collected evaders and sent them in small groups across the Pyrénées. Betrayed by one of her own helpers, Gertrude ended up in Ravensbrück Concentration camp. The work of the Marie-Claire line was taken over by Comptesse de Saint Venant whose code name was Marie-Odile.

fellow prisoner; he was one of the rare evaders who had crossed the Pyrénées on his own, only to be thrown into gaol by the Spanish militia. Ultimately they all travelled to Madrid and then Gibraltar to be flown to England via Marrakech.

Marie-Odile was arrested on 4th May 1944, with several members of her organisation; she suffered terrible torture and died in deportation at Ravensbrück camp.

On 25th January 1944, at 12.30pm, the Gestapo arrested the Delavignes. They were taken to Maréchal Foch Square in Nantes and immediately separated for interrogation. Tantine never saw her husband again; she eventually heard from other prison inmates that he had been taken to Compiègne, a transit camp controlled by the German army for the internment of political prisoners. On 29th March, he and many others were packed naked into a slatted cattle wagon with no food or water. The wagon was kept locked for the duration of the journey that took three to four days to reach Mauthsusen. Here he was kept in quarantine before being sent to Camp No. 1 at Gusen where the conditions were so appalling that he was unable to keep going through the terrible privations of the concentration camp. He died of exhaustion in January 1945.

The Germans were particularly keen to find out the motivation behind Mme. Delavigne's trip to Poitiers; she refused to tell them, and was kept in the cellars of the German Police headquarters for sixteen hours with fetters on her ankles and with her hands shackled behind her back. To try to get her husband cleared, Tantine then made up a long story with no names involved.

She had to endure two more interrogation sessions; for the last one she was held in the cellars for thirty hours, during which time she could hear the screams of the Frenchmen who were being tortured nearby. She determinedly refused to give her interrogator, Dr. Rupert (Head of the Gestapo), any of the names or details he demanded, so he repeatedly slapped her face and then said; 'in Germany we respect women, but I shall treat you as a man and I shall put it out of your power to do us harm. You are going into a concentration camp until the cessation of hostilities.'

Tantine was taken to the prison at Romainville, a military installation east of Paris. There was an ambience of warm friendship amongst the prison gang, and this sustained the women while they were incarcerated here. They were then incarcerated in other places throughout the war or until they died. However, this was one of the main transit points to Nazi concentration camps, and in due course Tantine was transported to Germany, at which point Dr.Rupert informed her eighty-two-year-old blind mother that she would have to get out of her house within two days and that he himself would occupy the apartment as a reprisal for the family's work against Germany. Tantine then journeyed via the prisons of Aix-la-Chappelle, Dusseldorf, Hanover and Hamburg. She arrived in Ravensbrück on 21st March 1944.

There is no firsthand account of Tantine's experiences in Ravensbrück, but many of the political prisoners wrote testimonies of their time in this appalling place. Cattle trucks would complete the long journey, arriving at a station which served the health resort at Fürstenberg, usually in the middle of the night. Here the prisoners were unloaded and were confronted by guards with dogs tugging at their leashes in a terrifying manner. They were forced to walk to the camp where the hapless women were herded together and made to stand until morning in the cold night air. At 5am, a siren sounded and all the existing prisoners were marched out into the open to line up in blocks of five, standing erect with their hands by their sides while the long count took place. They then returned inside where a daily ration of so called coffee was doled out, together with a lump of bread. A second siren would sound as a signal for these prisoners to march off to work. The newcomers were ordered to strip, and everything was taken from them including all personal possessions. Ordered to shower and submit to shaving of their heads and pubic hair, they were then issued with prison garments with a number sewn on the sleeve; this number was to become the only identity by which they would be known. Political prisoners had a red triangle sewn above the number. Many of these were designated 'NN', and were destined to disappear into the night and fog with no identity, even in death.

The following procedure was adopted for choosing the factory workforce. In the company of SS guards, representatives of the manufacturers came to choose their workers. They felt the prisoners' muscles and examined their faces to check on their health, and then they selected the ones they wanted. Then each prisoner was made to walk naked past the doctor and he eventually decided if a woman was fit to work in the factories. The work they were detailed to do was exhausting, mainly because of lack of food and sleep; in addition to twelve solid hours of work, everyone had to take part in the roll call each morning and evening. Ravensbrück was a slave labour camp where the prisoners were overworked until they died.

One would hope that Tantine was employed as a nurse like the Comptesse de Milleville (code named Marie-Claire) who also survived her time at Ravensbrück. As such, the conditions for their work and their living conditions would have been marginally better than for those who had been selected for slave labour.

Out of the blue on the morning of 2nd March 1945, a siren summoned all the prisoners to march past the SS guards. The sound of cannon fire could be heard in the distance as the Soviet Army approached. The guards directed the prisoners into two lines. Tantine was on the move again; she was one of a group of prisoners taken to Mauthausen concentration camp near Linz in Austria. Mauthausen was close to Gusen, where Adrien Delavigne had been sent. These two camps were the only camps to belong to the Grade 3 category, punishment camps for the 'incorrigible political enemies of the Reich', used for extermination through labour of the intelligentsia from the countries that Germany occupied during the war. The prisoners did heavy work on a starvation diet; they lived for an average of two to three months.

By the time Tantine arrived at Mauthausen, the massive overcrowding was causing dreadful problems; malnutrition, typhus and other illnesses were the cause of hundreds of deaths.

Andrée Dumon, 'Nadine', was still very young when she was captured while working for the Comet Line. She was interviewed by Martyn Cox many years later. Like Tantine, she was designated NN and was supposed to just disappear. The following is a transcription from spoken words:

'So where were you, when the war ended you were still in a camp?' Martyn asked her.

'Yes', she replied, 'In a very, very bad place, because I was not working and I was not very well, so they were sent, a lot of prisoners were sent in a valley, in a quarry, you know, a quarry, but we didn't work there. But there is only a roof, a place, a roof, a mattress on the ground, no water, no light; the toilets are outside at, je ne sais pas quoi, 50 metres or more. So in the night you have to go because we are all ill. So it's always people go and come in. It's awful. Nearly no eat and if we want to wash ourselves, it's a little river, you understand, but the toilets of the Germans go in the river, so! That was clearly awful.'

'So how did your time in the camp finish? Did the Allies come and release you?'

'No, no. It's on the 22nd of April because I never wrote something, but some dates I never forget. So, when I was arrested, when I was liberated, 22nd April '45.

But because the French Government took an agreement with the International Red Cross and they asked to take the French prisoners in Mauthausen, in that camp, Mauthausen, and then the Red Cross came to Mauthausen but there were not enough French, so they take also Belgians. So otherwise maybe I shall not be here because I was very, very ill in the end. Everybody thought I should die'.

As early as October 1944, the International Council of the Red Cross warned the German Foreign Office of the impending collapse of the German transportation system due to the Allied bombing campaign. The ICRC considered that starvation conditions for people throughout Germany were becoming inevitable. In February 1945, the Canadian Red Cross donated a number of Chevrolet Canadian Military Pattern trucks and the German Government agreed to give Canadian Prisoners of War parole so that they could drive supply trucks to the POW camps to deliver food supplies.

Early in March, there was a meeting between Carl Burckhardt and SS Ober-gruppenführer Ernst Kaltenbrunner who was the head of the Reich Security Main Office, and was overseer of all the concentration camps. Immediately after this, there were negotiations between Adolf Windecker and Fritz Berber, Joachim von Ribbentrop's representative to the ICRC. The main subject of discussion was the exchange of French internees in Germany for German internees held in France. The discussions soon came to a standstill. This prompted the ICRC to dispatch a special representative, Hans E. Meyer, to Berlin, where he had very good contacts; this resulted in a meeting with Himmler. This in turn led to an agreement for the transportation of 299 French and one Polish female detainee from Ravensbrück to Switzerland, in exchange for the release of 454 German civilians in France.

After the first of these prisoners had been repatriated, the roads between Northern and Southern Germany closed due to the Allied bombings; this made it impossible to organise another convoy for Ravensbrück, so in order to make up the agreed numbers the ICRC were then able to arrange three deportee convoys from Mauthausen.

On 21st April, a Red Cross representative arrived in the Mauthausen camp. Commandant Franz Ziereis cooperated with the removal of a number of French, Belgian and Dutch prisoners. Tantine was one of the French prisoners to be liberated the following day by the ICRC.

A number of the Canadian Red Cross trucks were used to transport Tantine and her compatriots from Mauthausen to Switzerland. Huge problems arose for the first

4 ~ TANTINE'S WAR

convoy when it reached Switzerland; the border was closed by the Swiss authorities from 5pm to 10am the following morning. The former detainees were forced to spend the night on the road, without blankets, hot drinks or food. There was a lack of sanitary facilities and shelter. The women were then transferred onto trains and taken to the refugee centre at St. Gall. The total journey was well over three hundred miles. Sadly, some of them were so ill that they did not survive the journey and a few of the others died in the hospital in spite of the best efforts of the medical staff. In testimony written while at St. Gall, one of the survivors who left the camp on 24th April later wrote that the trucks were waiting 500 metres from the camp but the prisoners were kept in the freezing cold for four hours before they were allowed to board them.

The one time Benedictine Abbey at St. Gall had a long tradition of sheltering the traveller and providing a rudimentary hospital for the sick until the secularization and closure of the monastery in 1805. The Canton of St. Gall was built on the lands previously owned by the Monastery, located in the north eastern corner of Switzerland bordering on Austria.

The centre was administered by the Swiss Red Cross with the help of local army reservists and the gendarmerie. Together they offered the survivors food, clothing, shelter and basic medical care. St. Gall became the transit hub for several large groups of concentration camp survivors sent to Switzerland near and after the end of the war for recovery and medical treatment. There were four facilities where medical treatment was available.

With the exception of those who needed hospitalisation, these prisoners were then taken to the Annecy centre, which was just over the border in France. From there, Tantine still had to face a five hundred mile journey to her home in Nantes on the other side of the country.

On her return Tantine weighed just four and a half stone, (28.5 kg); her normal weight was ten stone (63.5 kg).

65

5

THE FRENCH RESISTANCE

About twenty years ago, John spoke to some schoolchildren about his wartime helpers:

'Recently I was present at a meeting of the Escaping Society in Brussels, celebrating the anniversary of the setting up of the Comet Line, a very successful escape organisation organised by the Belgians. In his sermon, the British chaplain drew attention to the fact that as he reads stories and talks to people year by year he never ceases to wonder at how ordinary they are but when difficult situations crop up for them how they then meet extraordinary situations with calm and wit; they were nurses, teachers, gardeners, in some cases interpreters for the Germans, post office engineers, masons and whatever. I was helped by such people during the war. They were magnificent people, but quite ordinary people who rose to the challenges of war in extraordinary ways.'

In 1940, Marcel Hévin was a 34 year old married man with two children. He worked as a designer/draftsman with the SNCF, the national railway, in Nantes. He was a considered and calm man who found the German occupation unbearable, so he decided to do something about it. He recruited some young people from the local area of La Marrhonnière in Nantes. In August 1940 he was working to help provide false papers to these young people so that they could travel to the free zone and then on to England to join the Free French Forces (FFL). The group obtained photographs of the airbase at Château Bougon and kept a log of all the local troop movements, this information was passed to Captain Dewavrin, alias 'Passy', of General De Gaulle's staff in London.

The Nazi authorities were determined to prevent any trouble on Armistice Day, 11th November 1940. They forbade all ceremonies, including church services, but students in Paris staged a huge protest against the occupation and paraded along the Champs-Élysées. In Nantes, the young members of the Marcel Hévin group went to the cemetery of La Gaudinière and placed flowers on the graves of British soldiers. On this day they appointed Marcel Hévin as their leader. He operated under the code name 'Patt' and became involved in sheltering and helping a number of soldiers and airmen return to England.

The Regional Chief Engineer of the SNCF was M. Turban of Rennes, who was one of the organisers of La Bande à Sidonie, later integrated into the Georges France 31 network with direct links to the Intelligence Service in London. Marcel Hévin gathered the notes on troop movements and all relevant military information and passed this to M. Turban.

Sadly, the close connection between the various groups was a direct cause of their decimation once the first infiltrations were followed by the inevitable denouncements. However, there was no connection between these groups and the French Communist resistance fighters who were fighting against fascism but their loyalty was to the Allies fighting with the Soviet Union, not to France and General de Gaulle. They believed that their cause was best served by assassinating senior German officers.

An agent of the Abwerh, André Barrault, managed to infiltrate the Veper group, which liaised with the Hévin group; as a result of this Marcel Hévin was arrested at his workplace on 25th April 1941. There was no evidence against him but he was held in prison then transferred to Fort Romainville. He was one of the hostages who were shot in reprisal for the assassination of Lieutenant Colonel Karl Hotz, the Feldkommandant (German military governor) of Nantes on 20th October 1941.

Lieutenant Colonel Hotz had led a team of German engineers and labourers from Düsseldorf working in the city of Nantes during the years before the war and was considered to be a Francophile. Hotz did his best to protect the people of Nantes from the worst aspects of the occupation, but early in the morning of 20th October he was assassinated while he was walking to work. Hitler initially thought that this was the action of British agents and he demanded the immediate execution of at least a hundred hostages. A curfew was imposed and a reward of up to one million francs was offered for information leading to the arrest of the assassins. On 22nd October, sixteen hostages were shot at Nantes, another 27 at Chateaubriant and still more at Mont-Valerian outside Paris, bringing the total to 48. The reprisals came as an enormous shock to many Bretons. Their faith in Marshal Petain's promises of protection was shaken.

Mme. Marie-Louise Huau owned the Boîte à Sardines restaurant in the Rue Bellamy. On hearing of the reward that was on offer, she told the French Police that two men who she hadn't seen before had been eating in her restaurant in the days before 20th October but had not appeared on the following two days. She was questioned by the Gestapo and recognised Gilbert Bruslein in a photograph they showed her. The truth soon came to light. Three communist resistance fighters, Marcel Bourdarias, Gilbert Brustlein and Spartaco Guisco, had travelled to Nantes with the intention of assassinating German officers; there had been no local involvement at all. Mme. Huau claimed her reward after Gilbert Brustlein and Spartaco Guisco were arrested by the Gestapo. The two men were tortured and then executed. Gilbert Brustlein was never found.

La Bande à Sidonie, an intelligence gathering network, was created by Suzanne Wilborts, a midwife who was married to Dr. Adrein Wilborts, a paediatrician who had been burned by gas in the trenches in World War 1. In 1936 he retired and moved the family to the Cotes d'Armor in Bréhat. Their young daughter Marie-José was a medical student who had a pass to travel home at weekends, she carried back details of coastal defence plans hidden in her college books. In Rennes she would pass the information to her contact André, either at the Café de l'Europe or the Café de la Paix.

Suzanne found many ingenious ways of conveying information; a letter she sent to General de Gaulle offering her services was hidden in a toy duck that was wheeled across the border by a toddler travelling with his mother to join his sailor father. The success of the group came to an end when it was infiltrated and all the members were imprisoned in May 1942.

Jean-Baptiste Legeay entered the Congregation of the Brothers of Christian Instruction in Phoërmel at the age of 16. His novitiate took place in England, at Bitterne, near Southampton. On completion of his studies he made his Profession of Faith and took the name Brother Clair-Marie. In September 1914, he returned to France and started teaching. He was called up in August 1918 and was sent to the front with the 45th Artillery Regiment at Orléans. On 9th June 1918, Jean-Baptiste Legeay was severely injured. He was hospitalised for some time and after his recovery he remained in military service with the Franco-American division at the headquarters in Orléans.

Between the wars, Jean-Baptiste Legeay perfected his command of English when he spent some time at the Theological College at Pell Wall in Birmingham. He was then appointed headmaster of the secondary school in Nantes-Chantenay, and when France fell he was the director of day pupils at the Saint-Similien School in Nantes. He created a youth club for the students and meetings took place after Mass on Sunday mornings. The students were in their late teens and they talked to him about their thoughts and ideas and sought his help to find a way of defeating the occupiers. Many thought that they should somehow get to England to enrol in the Free French Forces. He advised them to stay put as there was plenty for them to do at home. Resistance was a bit like a game to them and they were not really aware of the dangers involved; the risk of being arrested towards the end of 1940 was pretty low. Brother Legeay collected intelligence about fuel convoys and the presence of painted wooden aeroplanes in the south of the Château-Bougon area; these were designed to fool the RAF observation aeroplanes. He taught the students to make careful records of the badges and insignia of the German units stationed in the area. On one occasion, a patriot gave him a set of defence plans that he had managed to procure.

Once Brother Legeay was passing intelligence information to La Bande à Sidonie, it was not long before he was also helping the Marcel Hévin group with their work, which included assisting escapers and evaders to find shelter and a route to the UK. He was an honest and outspoken man who was not afraid to show his opinion of the Germans; his patriotism was obvious to anyone who came into contact with him. This brought him to the attention of the occupying forces and consequently he was soon under surveillance so his superiors transferred him to the Postulancy of Roscoat in Pléhédel, in the Côtes-du-Nord. Here his activities focused more and more on assisting evaders and escapers.

In December 1941, Hitler had issued the infamous 'Nacht und Nebel' decree. The name had originated during the previous century, in the writings of Johann Wolfgang von Goethe describing clandestine actions hidden by dark night and fog. This decree allowed for prisoners suspected of endangering German security to disappear; they were abducted in secret and deported to Germany where they were interrogated and then sentenced by special courts. The authorities then carried out the sentence by execution or transfer to concentration camps, where these prisoners were known only by a number, and their jackets were marked with the letters NN. They were prevented from having any contact with family or friends and effectively just vanished into the night and fog.

The three men at the centre of John's initial contact with the French Resistance were denounced and arrested. For providing assistance to the crews of two Allied aircraft, they were tried by a German military tribunal in Paris and then taken to Germany where they were beheaded with an axe.

George Le Bonniec was arrested on 5th March 1942; Edouard Andre Marchais was arrested on 1st July. They were both beheaded on 20th October. Jean Baptiste LeGeay was arrested on 13th November, and on 10th February 1943, his 46th birthday, he was beheaded in Cologne.

Suzanne Wilborts and her daughter were imprisoned, together with the entire group on 22nd May 1942. The women were transported from Paris Gare de l'Est by convoy on 26th July. They eventually arrived in Ravensbrück, where they remained until the beginning of March 1945 when they were amongst thirty women transferred to Mauthausen. This was at the same time as Tantine. On 22nd April, they were liberated by the Swedish Red Cross. It was only when they returned to France that Suzanne and Marie-Jo learned of the death of Dr. Adrien Wilborts in Buchenwald concentration camp on 24th February 1944.

When Stanislaus Ryps left John, he must have struck out on his own; somewhere along the line he was captured and interrogated. He was brought to Bordeaux where the Germans determinedly broke him down to obtain all the information he held. Solitary confinement, near starvation and repeated brutality would challenge the strongest character, and he had, over the previous months, shown himself to be of a naturally nervous disposition.

In February 1942 two German agents arrived at Mme. Mahé's house and told her that they were friends of Ryps, and that he had asked them to collect some items of his so that they could bring them to him. She told them that she was not acquainted with anyone of that name. One of them told Mme. Mahé that he needed somewhere to stay and she sent them to see Mlle. Raux who could not help, so they continued to Mme. Rigaud's house where they asked for butter. When Mme. Mahé gave her testimony after the war, she said that this was the fateful conversation in which Mme. Rigaud let slip that she knew about Ryps. The consequences of those few words were far reaching; thankfully John did not have to cope with the knowledge of any of this until it all came to light, piece by piece, in the years after the war. Many of the people who were implicated were deported to Germany; only a few returned in 1945. Mme. Mahé was taken to the Rue des Rochettes, a German military prison. From here she was transferred to the Saint-Jean fort in Bordeaux where she remained for several months before she was released with no conviction.

STREET NAME MEMORIAL TO ADRIEN DELAVIGNE IN NANTES
COURTESY OF DAVE FURNISS

NANTES MEMORIAL TO MARCEL HEVIN AND HIS EXECUTED COMRADES.

6

THE FORT
DE LA REVÈRE

In France, the occupied and unoccupied zones were separated by the demarcation line. Italy had declared war on France on 10th June 1940, and had made a few gains between then and when the Franco-Italian armistice was signed on 24th June. When two armistice commissions came into being, it was agreed that Italy's troops would now occupy these small areas and in addition the Franco-Italian Commission would deal with the area of the unoccupied zone east of the Rhône River, while the rest came under the Franco-German Commission.

The Italian commissioner had given permission to use the Fort de la Revère as a prison, subject to the guarantee that no escapes would occur. Modifications took place over the course of the first two months of 1942. Entrance to the fort was over a large drawbridge, beyond which was a covered passageway, leading to the area that was to become the exercise area/parade ground. At either end of this, new latrines were built, that were to be emptied regularly by horse and cart; the original latrines had been constructed with pipes that led into the moat but this was now dry. The area for the prisoners was enclosed by a high barbed wire fence, and the underground passages were all blocked off. Washrooms and kitchens with barred windows were situated below the living quarters, looking out over the moat. The living quarters themselves were situated under a thick layer of soil, with ventilation shafts to the air above. High arc lights were installed with guard lookout posts strategically placed on the perimeter.

When John reached the Fort de la Revère, in June 1942, he found himself in the company of about two hundred and fifty prisoners, who had been detained in France for anything up to two years. These were evaders and escapers who had made their way into the unoccupied zone of France. According to international law, the evaders should have been interned until the end of the war, but the escapers were free to make their way back to their own country and back to the war. Evaders knew that they needed to have an escape story ready in case of capture. However, the Vichy authorities were obliged to detain them all, owing to the existence of Article 10 in the Armistice Convention that had been signed on 22nd June 1940. Many of the group John met had originally come together when they were held in Marseilles. Early in 1941, they had been moved inland to a more secure environment at Saint Hippolyte du Fort. At this time, the group became known as Detachment W. In March 1942, after a search to find a fortress offering totally secure internment, they were transported to the Fort de la Revère.

Six downed airmen were transferred to the fort on 1st May. Then, on 15th May, they were joined by Pilot Officer Tadeusz Wawerski and Sergeant Stephan Miniakowski, of 300 Squadron. Stephan Minialowski was transferred to hospital and successfully escaped. Teddy Wawerski and John became friends, and it seems likely that he was the Polish friend who took John's twisted florin, and crafted it into a small silver aeroplane that stayed with John until his eventual return to England.

The fort was overcrowded and the few officers did their best to make life as comfortable as possible. They negotiated with their captors and the prisoners were allowed to purchase radio sets from a shop in nearby Nice. The occupants of each room bought one so that they could listen to the news from London. The long term prisoners were dressed in worn-out clothing of all types, and an appeal had gone out to the Red Cross to send uniforms. This suited Commandant Digoine and his staff, because anyone escaping could be spotted easily if they were wearing uniform. Each man was issued with a battle-dress uniform, a forage cap, a pair of boots, shirts and underwear. One outside visitor, who John remembered visiting the fort, was the young Prince Raniere of Monaco. The Principality of Monaco was situated on the coast below the fort, and its ruler, Prince Raniere's grandfather, gave his loyalty to Marshall Petain, who had been his friend and compatriot in the First World War. However, Prince Raniere was pro-Allied, and at this time was waiting to reach his majority so that he could serve with the Free French Forces.

At John's request, the Prince arranged for a supply of needles and embroidery silks for the men. The instructions were given for the men to embroider the service insignia onto the new uniforms, and this task was completed in time for the next church parade.

Complaints about the food were countered with the assurance that the men were better fed than the population at large. Fortunately, Red Cross parcels were delivered regularly. The Joint War Organisation of the British Red Cross and The Order of Saint John packed and sent 20 million parcels over the course of the war. Whenever possible they contained:

- 1/4lb packet of tea
- tin of cocoa powder
- bar of milk or plain chocolate
- tinned pudding
- tin of meat roll
- tin of processed cheese
- tin of condensed milk
- tin of dried eggs
- tin of sardines or herrings
- tin of preserve
- tin of margarine
- tin of sugar
- tin of vegetables
- tin of biscuits
- bar of soap
- tin of 50 cigarettes or tobacco (sent separately)

In the knowledge that the prisoners would have to depend largely on the British Red Cross Society for food, it was decided early in the war that, so far as any clandestine work was concerned, no attempt should ever be made to get contraband articles into the camps under the protection of Red Cross labels. The use of next of kin parcels was also banned, since they were sent under the auspices of the Red Cross. This rule was never broken.

John was always determined to boost morale whenever possible. During his stint as Mess Officer, when the only fresh food for a number of weeks turned out to be a daily delivery of black bread, plus one sack of onions and one sack of potatoes, he prided himself on designing more than seven variations of menus, so that the tedious repetition of the same meal each day was alleviated. When I was a child, he would gently chide me with this story if I was reluctant to eat the food in front of me.

There was a stove in the centre of each room in the overcrowded accommodation at the fort. Even in early summer, the rooms became cold once the sun went down. Escorted parties of men were taken out of the fort to collect wood and pine cones to fuel the stoves. One Alsatian officer took it upon himself to escort the officers to bathe in the sea each day. The group would head off via a little, poorly defined path, 3,000 feet down to the water. The plunge into the water was blissful, but the price they had to pay was the extremely difficult climb back up to the top. However, they were aware that the exercise was a good way of keeping fit in preparation for any opportunity to escape.

One of the French officers was fond of English tea and asked if he might buy some from the Red Cross supply. Knowing that the French were inclined to favour weak tea, they traded some for brandy, but only after they had already used the tea for two brews, then dried the leaves off.

On his arrival at the fort, John had officially become a Prisoner of War. On 15th June he sent the following postcard to his parents in Wallington. At least this time they did not have quite such a long wait for news after the dreaded telegram, which they had received on 29th May:

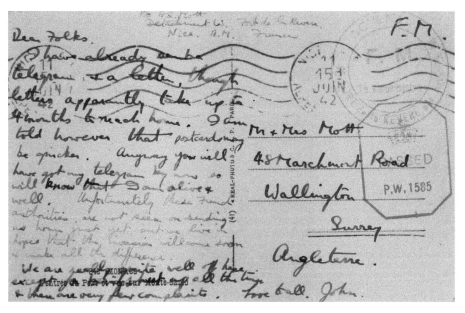

JOHN'S PARENTS RECEIVED THE FIRST NEWS OF HIS WHEREABOUTS.
AUTHOR'S COLLECTION

PT.O. A. J. MOTT DETACHMENT
W. FORT DE LA REVÈRE, NICE. A.M. FRANCE

Dear Folks

I have already sent a telegram and a letter, though letters apparently take up to 4 months to reach home. I am told however, that postcards may be quicker. Anyway you will have got my telegram by now so will know that I am alive and well, Unfortunately these French authorities are not keen on sending us home just yet, but we live in hope that the invasion will come soon and make all the difference. We are really quite well off here except for being so fed up all the time and there are very few complaints.

Postmarked 15 June 1942
Mr and Mrs Mott
48 Marchmont Road
Wallington
Surrey
Angleterre
Love to all, John

John's fiancée Whynifred had found a new love interest during his second protracted absence and, at some point during his time as a POW, he received news of this in what was aptly named a 'Dear John' letter.

The time when the bulk of the prisoners had been collected together in Marseille had been at the beginning of an organised escape line, which eventually became known as the PAT Line. Alex Nitelet had been delivered by John to take up the position as wireless operator for the PAT Line and he and John were to nearly come together again before too long.

The Reverend Donald Caskie had left his Scottish Church in Paris, just ahead of the Germans, and had taken over the Seaman's Mission at 46 Rue de Forbin in Marseille, on the understanding that it was only to be used for civilian refugees. Food and funding came in from anonymous individuals. Food was left in the doorways of the mission at night, and anonymous telephone calls gave notice of police checks. Uniforms were collected by Caskie, placed in a sack with rocks, and dropped into Marseille Harbour at night. Having joined forces with Ian Garrow, an escape line had evolved, and escapers and evaders now started to move from Northern France to Marseille, then over the Pyrénées, and on to Gibraltar.

Belgian Army doctor Albert-Marie Guerisse had served as a Captain with a Belgian cavalry regiment, but when his country capitulated, he escaped and managed to sail from Dunkirk to Margate. He was commissioned in the Royal Naval Volunteer Reserve. Whilst on a clandestine operation off the coast of France, he capsized and was later captured and imprisoned in St. Hippolyte du Forte; from here, he escaped and made his way to Marseille, where he joined the resistance. He worked tirelessly to assist evading airmen and others through the escape lines. He took the name of a Canadian friend, Patrick Albert O'Leary, and was generally known as Pat O'Leary. When Garrow was arrested in October 1941, O'Leary took over command of the escape line, which became known as 'the PAT Line'.

Another early key helper was Dr. Georges Rodocanachi (known as Rodo). He had been born in Liverpool, spent his school days in Marseille, was educated in Paris, and was of Greek parentage. Together with his wife Fanny, and their elderly maid Seraphine, he ran the line's main safe house in Marseille, at 21 Rue Roux de Brignoles, using his doctor's surgery as a collecting house for evaders. This address later became the headquarters of the PAT Line.

On 22nd June, Squadron Leader Whitney Straight and Sergeant Stephan Miniakowski, together with Private Knight of the Dorsetshire Regiment, escaped from the Pasteur

Hospital in Nice and were assisted back to England by members of the PAT Line. Whitney Straight was a highly decorated RAF pilot and a famous Grand Prix motor racing driver. He kept his identity secret, and contrived to fake an illness, so that he could attempt an escape from the hospital. During his time as an internee he was known as Captain Whitney.

MI9 were anxious to get experienced pilots safely back to England, and had asked Patrick O'Leary to assist with the escape of Frederick Higginson, known as 'Taffy'. He was using the name Captain Basil Bennett RAOC, from the time when he was first held in Marseille. He was one of many who disguised their RAF background, as it was understood that the Germans were particularly anxious to prevent any of the airmen from escaping and they were determined to transfer them to POW camps in Germany whenever possible.

After Witney Straight's escape, Taffy Higginson was now the Senior British Officer (SBO) and he had been busy planning an escape. There were a number of useful contacts on the outside, and Taffy and Pat O'Leary had already known each other since the time when Paul Cole had escorted Taffy to the home of Dr. Rodocanachi in Marseilles. Impatient with the delay in plans to get him back to England, Taffy had made his own arrangements but was caught by the gendarmes with false papers. He eventually ended up at the fort. In Monte Carlo, the local basketball coach was a white Russian émigré called Vladimir Bouryschkine, who went under the name of Val Williams. He queried the provision of exercise for the prisoners, as laid down by the Geneva Convention, and eventually persuaded the Vichy authorities to let him make regular visits to the men inside as a PT instructor. His bi-weekly sessions became such a normal part of the routine that, after a while, the guards did not bother to search him. Another useful visitor was the Polish Catholic priest, Father Myrda. He would arrive with a large bag full of religious parapher-nalia to enable him to celebrate Mass, so it was comparatively simple for him to slip in a few small tools to assist the prisoners with their escape plans. The fort's interpreter, Mr Wood, could also be relied on to carry verbal messages backwards and forwards.

The Reverend Donald Caskie had helped many evaders and escapers during his time at the Seamen's Mission in Marseille. Ultimately he had been brought before a Vichy military tribunal and instructed to close the Seamen's Mission and to move away. The suggested destination was Grenoble. From there, Donald Caskie was occasionally permitted to travel to the fort to minister to the POWs, many of whom he had known well in Marseilles. His journey was long and arduous and, on one occasion he was weighed down by a large sack, so he was feeling tired as he toiled up the hill towards the fort. He heard the sound of a goose behind him and turned to see a boy struggling with an uncooperative bird. He put down the sack and went to help the boy. Under cover of trying to calm an aggressive goose, the boy greeted him by a nickname that Pat O'Leary had given him – 'Le Canard', after the character Donald Duck. Scuffling with the goose, the pair of them had by now moved off the path and out of the line of sight of anyone at the fort. The boy now imparted the message which had been sent by Pat O'Leary via Mr Wood. It was a warning that the sack would be searched. Hidden among the hymn books, Communion chalices, cigarettes and chocolate were forged ration books and passports, together with some small crowbars. The boy took control of the goose and continued on his journey.

Donald Caskie grabbed his sack and stumbled down the bank towards the stream below where he hid the sack in the undergrowth. Then, he started clambering up the slope away from the stream and towards the fort. Unexpectedly, he found a sewer exit hidden beneath a large overhanging bush. This obviously led to the camp and belonged to the disused sewer system. He hurried up to the camp hoping that his detour had not been observed. Arriving at the entrance, he was surrounded, and marched into the presence of the Commandant. After a thorough search and some angry words, he was permitted to hold the service but was under close watch throughout. Mr Wood doubled up as the organist for these services and while he was playing the harmonium as loudly as he could, Donald Caskie passed on the details of the position of the sewer exit.

Plans were soon underway for a breakout, before the Italian military authorities could arrange to move Detachment W somewhere even more secure. The fort was difficult to heat, and it was not practical to keep the prisoners there through the winter. One of the officers had noticed a metal inspection cover in the floor of the moat and they surmised that this led to the sewer. In the meantime, a number of men were working on a tunnel, which they hoped to complete before plans to remove them all from the fort could be brought to fruition.

Heading up the Escape Committee, Taffy selected his team; Flight Lieutenant MG Barnett RNZAF and three other airmen, who had previously made an escape attempt from the fort, namely Flying Officer Brian Hawkins, Sergeant Derrick Nabarro and Sergeant Pat Hickton RNZAF, who was known as Hicky.

In one of the officers' rooms there was a coal chute lined with barbed wire that led down to the kitchen. Sergeant Melville Dalfond, RCAF, managed to make a key to open the door of the chute. The kitchen had a low window leading out to the moat. The men had saved all the string from their Red Cross parcels and made them into a rope. To prevent rope burns they made makeshift gloves out of old khaki caps. Then they acquired old pullovers to protect themselves from the barbed wire in the coal chute.

Alex Nitelet was due to act as a guide to the escapers once they made their way out of the old sewer. He was to be accompanied by Tony Friend, who was an Australian Inspector of Police in Nice. Tony rented an apartment above an empty shop from Mr Turner, a London hairdresser who had returned to England. This apartment was used as a safe house on a number of occasions. Food was provided by two elderly spinsters, the Trenchard sisters, who owned a nearby tea shop in Monte Carlo during the times that it was occupied by evaders.

The escape was timed for an hour before roll call, when the guards were usually not very active. The men inside the fort arranged a noisy concert as a diversion and to cover the sounds made by the escaping officers. Armed with a hacksaw, the men made it safely to the kitchen and discarded the pullovers. They sawed through three bars across the kitchen window, then lowered themselves, one by one, down onto the floor of the moat. They had to risk the light from the arc lamps, and they were in a direct line from the sentry box, which was why the diversion was essential for their success. Lifting the inspection cover, they found that they were indeed in the collecting chamber where the sewerage had, at one time, been delivered from the latrines within the buildings. Now they had to crawl through the pipe which led to the exit that Donald Caskie had discovered. Their way was blocked by some bars set into the brickwork, and they broke the hacksaw blade trying to remove them, but Derrick Nabarro managed to kick his way out and the others followed, one by one. Now very dirty and decidedly smelly, they were delighted to be out in the fresh air.

The alarm was raised almost immediately and their two guides were nowhere to be found. Alex Nitelet and Tony Friend had been arrested by a passing patrol and taken in for questioning. Tony Friend was able to use his police credentials to extricate them from the difficult situation, but they were unable to be of any use to the escapers who headed off towards Monte Carlo. However, they went astray and eventually hid up in some bushes while Brian Hawkins, who had the most convincing identity documents, tried to find his own way to the address they had been given. This was the tearooms in Monte Carlo where he hoped to make contact with Pat O'Leary. All went well, and he led Pat back to the waiting escapers, collecting clean clothes from various washing lines as they went. After a few days in a safe house, the five of them were on their way to Marseilles. They were eventually repatriated by sea to Gibraltar and then to England.

The remaining eight officers and four orderlies were taken from the fort, early the next morning, on 25th April, and they arrived at the Fort de la Duchère that evening. On 5th September there was a mass escape from the Fort de la Revère, with Sergeant Melville Dalfond organising the plan from the inside. As a result of these escapes, Commandant Digoine was dismissed from the army, and his post was taken by Captain Bouvetier.

7

ALEX NITELET,
AN UNSUNG HERO

Alexander Nitelet was born in Luttre, on 12th January 1915, and became a pilot in the Belgian Air Force in 1938. On 5th August 1940, he arrived in England and signed up for the RAF, and was one of fifty five Belgian pilots who served with No. 609 Squadron.

On 9th August 1941, the squadron was stationed at Gravesend when Alex flew a 609 Squadron Spitfire, on a bomber escort mission known as Circus 68, over the Pas de Calais. Wing Commander Douglas Bader was in command of a large number of Spitfires that initially flew fighter sweeps over Northern France. They then became a crucial part of the Circus Operations where a few bombers were protected by a large number of Spitfires. On this, his first operation, Alex was flying his Spitfire AB780, and claimed one Me109 before he was shot down by the 109 of Karl Borris of 6/JG 26. A splinter from a cannon shell pierced his right eye, and he couldn't see through the blood to attempt to bail out. He crash landed near the little village of Renty, and was badly injured when his aircraft overturned. He was one of eight Spitfire pilots shot down during this bomber escort mission, and he was the only one to get back to England before the war ended. Three pilots were killed outright, one died of his wounds and the other three became prisoners of war. Douglas Bader made a number of unsuccessful attempts to escape and return to England.

The Resistance and the PAT Line now became an integral part of Alex Nitelet's life. From the time of the beginnings of Department W, a successful escape line had been slowly but surely, helping evaders and escapers make their way back to where they were free to return to fight the war. Momentous and difficult situations were unfolding; these were to have far-reaching effects. At this time, the head of the PAT Line was Albert-Marie Guerisse, a Belgian doctor who assumed the identity of his French Canadian friend Pat O'Leary, in order to protect his family in Belgium. There were many concerns about one of the line's most successful couriers, and Pat had just returned from a significant meeting in Gibraltar, hell-bent on confronting the traitor. Patrick O'Leary had been introduced to his new wireless operator when he was at the strategy meeting in Gibraltar. The two men travelled together with the transmitting and receiving set. Pat was not enamoured by anything about this Belgian man, Ferière, otherwise known as Drouet. It soon emerged that he just wanted to find a way to rejoin his wife who lived near Marseille; he had left her behind when he was evacuated from Dunkirk with the British Expeditionary Forces. One of the seamen, who rowed the two men from the Tarana to the shore, later wrote that 'once the two passengers stepped ashore and moved up the beach, the older one turned round to call out his thanks, but the younger one panicked and tried to get back to the boat, which by now was already pulling away from the beach'. Ferière proved himself to be a total disaster; he was useless and terrified, but now posed a threat because, in a very short while, he knew too many people and addresses. Pat needed to find a way of sending him and his wife away just as soon as possible. However, the more pressing problem was to deal with Paul Cole.

Alex Nitelet had crash landed in a field belonging to a local farmer, named Louis Salmon, who rescued him from the stricken aeroplane, and took him to the home of Vincent Ansel, a member of Norbert Fillerin's Resistance organisation. Before the Germans arrived to remove the Spitfire, the defiant and brave locals brought some local school children to line up in the shape of the 'V' for victory, to pose for a photograph. The Fillerin family arranged shelter for Alex over the next two months and nursed him back to health. He was treated by Dr. Guy Delpierre, from nearby Fauquembergues and Dr. Houzel from Boulogne. His eye was the most worrying of his injuries but his body had taken a severe battering, and his wounds caused problems throughout his life. At one point, he was housed with Desiré Didry, a blacksmith and shoemaker, from St Omer. Here he was joined at the house for a brief while by Flight Lieutenant Denis

Crowley-Milling, who was another Spitfire pilot, downed during one of the Circus Operations.

Then, in late September, Sergeant Patrick Bell joined Alex, suffering from injuries sustained when his Spitfire crashed; Pat was treated by Dr. Delpierre then, in early October, they were both moved to Burbure, near Auchel, where a number of other evaders were hidden in houses throughout the area. Fernand Salingue, a local schoolmaster, was sheltering Flying Officer George Barclay, who had been shot down north east of St. Omer, and had been passed from house to house until he reached this tiny village of Burbure, where Fernand and his wife Elisa looked after him for two weeks. Fernand was now making plans for the group to travel to Marseille on the first major step of their route home. He held a dinner party for all of them on 10th October, and the following morning, Paul Cole arrived and informed them that the departure had been delayed. When Alex heard that they would be heading off in a week's time, he made the journey home to visit his mother. According to the 609 squadron log she chided him for only managing to shoot down one aircraft, but happily leant him some money before sending him off on the long route to return to his duties. Alex had had no access to any money since he left Tangmere on 28th May. Before the group commenced the journey, another pilot, Pilot Officer Oscar Coen joined them. His Spitfire had been hit by the debris from a train he had just attacked and he bailed out near Calais. He hurt both his ankles, but walked until he made contact with the local Resistance.

The party of thirteen airmen and soldiers in the care of three guides from the PAT Line were divided into small groups, and headed off from Burbure in different directions. The guides were Paul Cole, Madame Damerment and her fiancée Roland Lepers. At Bethune, Alex's group joined up with the rest on the train to Abbeville, where the Abbé Pierre Carpentier prepared false papers for them, so that they could cross over the river into Occupied France. He was the vicar at the Church of Saint Giles, living in a small house on Place du Cimitiere Saint-Gilles, behind the bomb-damaged church with his widowed mother. Abbeville was situated on the River Somme and was a crossing point into the occupied zone. Local residents needed a transit pass, known as an Ausweis, to travel backwards and forwards. They had to present this pass, together with their French national identity card, containing a photograph, to the sentries who manned the bridges across the river. Printing had been a peacetime hobby for the Abbé who, with his small printing press, had become a craftsman. Now he created faultless forged documents for the escape line.

Once safely across the bridge, the group boarded a train and travelled to Paris where some of them were accommodated in an apartment and others at the Hôtel Flamel in Les Halles. They all went out to dinner at the Chope de Pont Neuf, and on their return were propositioned by three young women; the hotel was, in fact, a brothel. The following day, another guide, the young Susanne Warenghem, now joined them. They caught a train to Tours, near the demarcation line, and here they found the station full of German troops, so they waited for a local train that was not too crowded and travelled to St Martin-le-Beau. One by one they crossed the tracks, and walked along a path down to the River Cher, where they met their Portuguese guide, who took them, after dark, across the river into Vichy France. They walked all night to Loches where they caught a bus to Chateauroux. Suzanne left them here, and the original group travelled on another train to Toulouse, then on an overnight train to Marseille. The exhausted group were delivered to Louis Nouveau's beautiful fifth floor apartment at 28a Quai de Rive Neuve, overlooking the harbour. It was 1st November, All Saints' Day and as is detailed in a number of accounts, it was bitterly cold. The airmen stayed in the apartment overnight and the others were accommodated elsewhere, before travelling to safe houses. Alex was in need of some medical treatment, but there were momentous things happening at Dr. Rodocanachi's house. The completion of this long journey to Marseilles marked the beginning of the end of the PAT Line.

The men who had been safely brought to Marseilles were duly grateful to their guides, though some of them found Paul Coles' bravado quite worrying. Neither Paul, nor those in his charge, had any concept that he was about to be unmasked by Pat O'Leary. Born into a dysfunctional East End family, Harold Cole had grown up on the streets of the impoverished area around his home. He earned the nickname Sonny Boy, and was determined to pass himself off as someone from less humble beginnings. He affected a mode of speech that was scattered with officer class expressions such as 'old boy', and he dressed in a manner to fit in with the persona he was anxious to acquire. No one has ever been able to define why he was so attractive to women, but he certainly knew how to show them a good time. It turned out that he lavished money on them, even though the money was not his and had been given to him in good faith, for the expenses incurred by the loyal and hardworking members of the escape line. A petty criminal, who had been in and out of gaol, he joined up at the outbreak of war, and served with the Royal Engineers, attached to the 4ᵗʰ Infantry Division, who went to France as part of the British Expeditionary Force. Having been promoted to the rank of sergeant, he had charge of the Mess fund, and he absconded with this money early in 1940. He settled in Lille, where he became a master of disguise, and passed himself off as a British officer and secret service agent. There is no doubt that he was a valuable and skilled organiser within the escape line, but a number of people did not like his tendency to be boastful, and some were always inclined to be wary of him. His palpable lack of honesty in financial matters began to ring alarm bells, but the powers that be saw him as an asset, and were reluctant to listen to any doubts voiced by those who worked closely with him. Eventually, it came to light that several large sums of money that Captain Garrow had given Cole, for François Duprez, had been used by Cole to pay for women and parties. By the time of the arrival of this large group in Marseille, Pat O'Leary had uncovered the details of Cole's embezzlement, and had brought François Duprez to Marseilles to confront him. Ian Garrow, the previous leader of the escape line, had recently been arrested and Pat O'Leary had become even more suspicious of Paul Cole as a result.

On the afternoon of 1ˢᵗ November, there were a number of people distributed in the various rooms of the large apartment, which had become the headquarters of the PAT Line. This was on the second floor of Number 21, Rue de Brignoles. The apartment was owned by Dr. Rodocanachi and his wife Fanny, who had helped countless evaders over the preceding months, and who were at the very heart of the organisation. Pat O'Leary and key members of his team were awaiting the arrival of Paul Cole. Mario Praxinos and Bruce Dowding were sitting with Pat, in the small back bedroom, while François Duprez was hiding in the adjoining bathroom, where he could hear everything that was said in the bedroom. Paul arrived and the debriefing commenced with Pat leading the conversation round to the matter of the funds that had been entrusted to Paul for François Duprez. Apparently unconcerned, Paul began to lie his way out of the situation, when François Duprez burst out of the bathroom to confront him. Paul fell to his knees and begged for forgiveness. Incensed, Pat O'Leary swung at Paul Cole, and hit him full on in the face, severely damaging his own hand in the process. A summary execution was in the air, but the men decided to lock the criminal in the bathroom while they decided on their course of action. Before they came to a firm conclusion, they heard a noise from the bathroom and, rushing in, saw Paul Cole disappearing through the window. The window was high above a courtyard, and there was an adjacent window leading into one of the other bathrooms. In a desperate but successful bid for freedom, Paul had leapt out of one window and into the next one. He then ran through the apartment, down the stairs and was out in the street before Bruce Dowding could make his way through from the back bedroom to the front door, without disturbing the other people who were distributed around the various rooms. Bruce needed to make his way discreetly through the building in order to maintain the aura of a doctor's treatment rooms, so that the neighbours would never guess the true nature of the reason behind the visitors' appointments. Thus Paul Cole had a head start, and was out of sight before Bruce reached the street. Soon after his escape, Paul commenced his long trail of destruction and betrayal.

On the morning of 2nd November, Patrick O'Leary arrived at Louis Nouveau's apartment with a swollen hand to question the airmen about their convoyeur. Alex was grateful to the man who had led them thus far and understandably, became distressed by the whole situation as he and George Barclay argued out their different opinions of Paul Cole that evening. Even many years after the war, there were a number of evaders who had nothing but praise for Paul Cole, who had escorted them so successfully, and they simply could not come to terms with the realities of the depths of his treachery as, slowly but surely, it all came to light. Airey Neave referred to Cole as 'the most selfish and callous traitor'.

It was now time for the group to split up, so the soldiers went on to Nîmes, and the airmen stayed with Louis Nouveau and his wife Renée for two nights, before all of them, except Alex and Oscar Coen, were escorted by train to Perpignan. Here they joined a party of five Poles, and with a Spanish guide crossed the mountains. They walked by night and hid up during the day, until they reached Figueras. Then, they travelled on a goods train to Barcelona where they reported to the British Consulate.

Alex required some treatment from Dr. Rodocanachi before he and Oscar Coen were taken across the Pyrénées, near Le Perthus and on to Barcelona where all the airmen were reunited. They continued their journey to Madrid and from there to Gibraltar.

In Gibraltar there were a number of evading airmen impatiently waiting for transport home. One of these was John Mott, in the process of negotiating a lift home. Alex and Oscar Coen were flown back to Plymouth on Christmas Day. Alex sent his squadron a belated Christmas card.

During his own debriefing sessions, acknowledging that he was unfit to fly at this time, Alex requested that he should return to France and assist the members of the PAT Line who had enabled his recovery and brought him safely back. Once he had completed the debriefing procedure, he made contact with his squadron, where news of his survival had reached his colleagues, when he arrived in Barcelona in December. On 6th January, they celebrated his return at The Musician's Arms in Dorrington. Alex was admitted to Saint Mary's Hospital in Paddington the following morning, where his injured eye was excised.

On recovery from the operation, Alex was briefed with plans for the PAT Line's involvement with the commencement of sea operations, initially from Port Miou, near Cassis. In due course, Alex was charged with delivering the completed plans to the leaders in Marseilles. He had completed his training as a replacement wireless operator for the PAT Line. His experience as a pilot meant that this was quite straightforward.

On disembarking from the stricken Lysander, Alex was assisted by the agent in charge of the ground party (chef de terrain), Claude Lamirault, aka Fitzroy. His primary concern was to deliver Alex Nitelet to the leaders of the PAT Line, who were waiting in desperate need of their new wireless operator and the plans he was carrying. Claude hurried away with his charge, and left his second-in-command, Pierre Hentic, to sort out the problems created by the unfortunate presence of the pilot and the Lysander.

Alex arrived in Marseille with money for the PAT Line, his wireless set, and plans for a sea evacuation. His first transmission did not go well as he was overcome by nerves. However, he soon hit his stride, operating from three different addresses in Marseilles. He also sometimes used Gaston Nègre's apartment in Nîmes. Gaston was a highly successful black marketer who had made contact with Alex at the end of his journey to Marseilles, and assisted him with the problem of getting his bulky equipment through the security check at the railway station. Gaston Nègre had a vast network of contacts, and after the failure of Ferière, he had produced an unemployed radio operator, Roger Gaston, who used to work at the airport in Nîmes. This meant that when Alex arrived there were two of them to carry out these duties, and this released Alex to be helpful in other ways. He soon became a trusted lieutenant in the organisation.

One of the vessels involved in these plans was HMS Tarana, which had been used once before for an MI9 operation in mid April when Patrick O'Leary and his new wireless operator had arrived at Canet Plage. HMS Tarana was a motor trawler that was converted for use in the sea evacuations. Under heavy disguise and with increased accommodation, she operated out of Gibraltar. At the start of the voyage she flew the white ensign. Once underway, under cover of darkness, the crew would hastily disguise themselves and the ship. They painted her to resemble a local fishing vessel, changed out of their uniforms, and flew the Portuguese national flag. This had to be completed during the night hours and then the whole procedure was reversed during the night before arrival in Gibraltar.

The main priority at this time was the sea evacuation due to take place on 14th June. This was a combined SIS/MI9 operation, with the felucca Seawolf delivering the passengers to transfer onto the destroyer HMS Middleton. They included Fitzroy, Claude Limirault and his wife, Denise, together with the failed PAT Line radio operator, Ferière and his wife.

In mid July, Alex Nitelet worked as a guide for Operation BLUEBOTTLE. This was the first sea evacuation specifically organised for the PAT Line. Alex took Whitney Straight and Stefan Miniakowski, who had escaped from the hospital near the Fort de la Rivière, to Coursan on the Thursday before the evacuation. He then walked them into the woods towards St Pierre and hid them in a cave in the Gorge du Loup, just a few miles from the beach at Saint Pierre. Leaving them in the cave, he walked back towards Coursan to guide some of the others to join them. He met up with his fellow guide, Alex Wattebled, who was accompanying a group that included the SOE agent André Simon. André was on his way back to deliver the papers entrusted to him when he had been released from prison. Late in the evening of the evacuation, Alex led them all to the beach where they waited for a torch signal from the Tarana. Alex responded with his torch, and a boarding party rowed in to collect the first eight passengers and to deliver some goods. The second part of the group was duly collected, and the Tarana headed for a rendezvous near Cassis to pick up the rest of her passengers, then she was homeward bound for Gibraltar.

The next major task for Alex was to help with the planned breakout of four officers from the Fort de la Revère. John Mott had arrived there at the end of May, and helped his fellow officers to plan their escape.

On the night of the escape, Alex was waiting outside the fort, together with Tony Friend, to guide the escapees on their way. Unfortunately, they were picked up by a police patrol, and it took all their powers of persuasion to talk themselves out of the situation. The fact that Tony Friend was employed by the Police Department must have helped.

On 27th August, Alex Nitelet was in Nîmes with Gaston Nègre, helping to receive a parachute drop of money and supplies. Unfortunately, the aeroplane overshot the drop zone before coming round again. As a result of the noise it created, the military were on their way to the scene before it was possible to clear away all the items that had been dropped. The four people on the ground were arrested and, in due course, Alex was imprisoned at le Fort de la Duchère in Lyons. On 5th November, he was moved to Chambaran, where he was thought to be a spy. Fortunately, John Mott was able to speak to the Commandant and identify him as an RAF pilot who John had known personally earlier in the war. Just a week later, the Germans occupied the South of France in Operation ATTILA, and there were intense discussions between the prisoners and the Commandant. John and his fellow inmates put forward a convincing argument that the Germans would shoot certain prisoners without any compunction. Alex was quietly released on 27th November, alongside eight others who were at risk from summary execution.

Back in the care of the PAT Line, Alex then made his way to Toulouse, where he met up with Ian Garrow, who had been sheltered at Françoise Dissard's house, since his rescue from Mauzac concentration camp on 6th December (Patrick O'Leary had smuggled a German uniform to him in his cell). Towards the end of January, Alex and Ian, together with two American evaders, were taken by a guide to Perpignan and across the Pyrénées into Spain, then onwards to the British Consulate in Barcelona where they arrived on 1st February. They were taken to Gibraltar on 5th February 1943 and were flown home together two days later.

Alex resumed his duties with the RAF in mid March. On 21st July he joined his Air Force friends to celebrate Belgian National Day. There was a special Te Deum at Westminster Cathedral, after which airmen and soldiers joined together for drinks at the bar of the Ritz Hotel. From here, the airmen gate crashed the official Belgian lunch at the Savoy, and celebrated late into the evening.

Alex's greatest wish was to return to his duties as a pilot, but had to content himself with operating thirteen missions as an air gunner/despatcher. Eventually, he was back at the controls as a pilot, flying specially adapted Hurricanes with ADLS, the Air Defence Letter Service. 1697 Flight operated out of Northolt; the pilots flew into airstrips in Normandy and picked up the mail, which had been brought from the front by despatch riders. On arrival at Northolt, a despatch rider would immediately collect the mail and take it to London, and by the time it was delivered to its destination, only four hours would have elapsed. Gradually this service spread to wherever the armies advanced in Europe.

When Belgium was liberated, in September 1944, Alex transferred to the Belgian Air Force Inspectorate. After the war, on 1ˢᵗ October 1946, he was discharged from the RAF to become part of the new Force Aérienne Belge. He attained the rank of Colonel Aviateur in 1969, ten years before his retirement.

Alex was forever grateful to the French people who had helped him to evade capture when his Spitfire was shot down; in due course he organised the presentation of commemorative medals to a number of those involved. He developed an enduring friendship with the Salmon family, and was Godfather to their daughter, Marianne.

The following awards were among the many decorations that Alex received:

Croix de Guerre 1940 avec Palme
Lion de Bronze
Chevalier de l'Ordre de la Couranne avec Palme
Chevalier de l'Ordre de Leopold avec Palme
Air Crew Europe Star
1939-45 Star
War Medal 1939-45

In the Belgian Congo in 1960, Colonel Avieteur Alex Nitelet was second in command as Adjunct to the Commander in Chief, General Gheysen. He retired through ill health in 1969, and died on 6ᵗʰ January 1981, at the military hospital in Nederover-Heembeek.

Colonel Alexandre Ermand Jules Ghislaine Nitelet is buried in the 'pelouse d'honneur' at the Cimetière de Woluwe-Saint-Lambert.

ALEX NITELET WITH HRH PRINCE BERNHARD OF THE
NETHERLANDS — COURTESY OF PHILIPPE MEERT

8

GUY LOCKHART; BRIGHTER THAN A SHOOTING STAR

WING COMMANDER W. GUY LOCKHART
COURTESY OF TANYA BRUCE-LOCKHART

Guy Lockhart was born in June 1916 in Richmond, Surrey. Two years later, his sister Evelyn was born. On 26th June 1920, at the age of three, he travelled to Shanghai, China on the P&O ship, SS Plassy. His father was listed on the passenger manifest as an accountant intending to live permanently in China.[3] At some point, not recorded, the family moved to Canada.

On 13th October 1926, now ten years old, Guy returned to England from Canada, with his mother and sister, on the SS Sarpedon of the Blue Funnel Line. His sister, Evelyn, contracted diphtheria and died a year later in Chelsea. Guy was educated at St. Vincent's Preparatory School for Boys in Eastbourne, East Sussex, and then at Sevenoaks School. His father returned to China and made a separate life there.

By the time Guy left school, tensions in Europe were rising, and in 1935 the Royal Air Force was expanding. On 21st October, now 19 years old, Guy enlisted on a Short Service Commission as Acting Pilot Officer. He was sent to No. 2 Flying School at Digby, and then posted to No. 6 Flying School at Netheravon in Wiltshire. On 31st August 1936, Guy was posted to No. 65 (F) Squadron at Hornchurch; he was confirmed in the rank of Pilot Officer two months later.

On 22nd March 1937, Guy was posted to No. 87 (Fighter) Squadron at Tangmere, flying the Hawker Fury, and in April he was training at the Armament Training Camp in North Coates Fitties. In July, the squadron was moved to Debden, and re-equipped with Gloster Gladiators.

In 1938, Guy's career with the RAF came to an untimely end, or so it seemed at the time. He was part of a display team flying Gloster Gladiators on Empire Air Day. There were displays across the United Kingdom showing off the skills of the pilots of the RAF for just one day of the year. The weather was poor initially, but the sun came out intermittently in the afternoon, and the crowd gathered at Stoke-on-Trent Municipal Airport looking up to the skies. In spite of the weather the crowd were thrilled to watch flight aerobatics by Gladiators, being performed with superb accuracy Unfortunately, Guy chose to show off his skill with a flamboyant low pass right over the heads of the VIP party, some of whom did not share his faith in his own ability. As a result, a few of them flung themselves to the ground as his aeroplane approached them. This incident resulted in a court martial. He resigned his commission in August, and became a flying instructor with the West Suffolk Aero Club.

---

3 The family had old links with Shanghai. Guy's great grandfather, William Lockhart MRCS, was a medical missionary who had founded a highly successful hospital in Shanghai in 1843. He later founded a hospital in Peking, and eventually returned to London where, for the remainder of his working life, he ran his practice in Blackheath.

Guy married Ruby Potter in Colchester early in 1939. Their daughter Tanya has provided the following account of their departure for their honeymoon. (My thanks to Joe Dible for his description of the Tiger Moth paraphernalia):

THE WEDDING PARTY

My mother, Judy Lockhart, as she became, was every bit as adventurous and feisty as my father; his sense of fun was a match for hers, although I think she sometimes found him reckless and audacious in his pursuit of adventure. They were both very young when they married during those pre-war days of sunshine and freedom in March 1939. I believe the wedding was a small affair but the decision to fly to Paris for the honeymoon was inspirational. My father had access to a Tiger Moth – one of those iconic biplanes, which were used as trainers both for the RAF and civil aviation. My father was a practised and skilled airman and an excellent flying instructor. Apparently, at the airfield before departure, he gave my mother strict instructions on how to manage matters 'should things go wrong'!

My mother had an overwhelming love for my father and trusted him implicitly. She and my grandmother had watched him loop the loop many times, without incident and were in awe of his aerobatic abilities. Although still in her wedding attire – including a most expensive frippery of a hat and lizard platform shoes – the new bride climbed into the aircraft completely enveloped in flying paraphernalia and with an enormous backpack of a parachute attached to her slender back.

The following description is courtesy of Joe Dible:

'The Tiger was a very draughty piece of kit, as the control cables left the cockpits through the side of the aeroplane and ran down the outside of the fuselage to the tail plane and some very nasty draughts came whistling in through the slots made in the side of the fuselage. So feet were permanently frozen and shoulders were also in the breeze. Some sort of fleece-lined boots were the norm for RAF pilots and the Sidcot jacket would have just appeared in use in 1939. This was named after Sidney Cotton, who flew clandestine missions over Germany in his private aeroplane, just prior to the war and was in fact taking many photos of likely targets in the event of war. He saw a need for pilots to keep warm in open cockpit trainers and this bulky fur-lined jacket was the result. So I think the lady would most likely have been wearing such a jacket but unlikely to have had the boots, as they simply would not have fitted over her wedding shoes!'

My grandmother, tethered to my father's English bull terrier, (who, as his canine companion had often flown with him) and the small attendant wedding guests, stood breathless as they watched the little biplane soar up into the sky and over the fields heading south, towards France. To my grandmother's horror, suddenly the Tiger Moth seemed to turn on its axis and a black speck began to tumble from its back, clinging to a swiftly opening parachute – my mother! The shocked wedding guests set forth across the fields to find my mother, clinging still to her feathery wedding hat, quite unharmed but somewhat shaken.

The story goes that my father, as he took the plane skywards, attracted my mother's attention and shouting above the noise of the engine, said something like "Alone at last" but mother, without a second's thought, imagined he was mouthing "Get out fast"! Her response was instant and her descent almost Bond-like in its accuracy!

Mummy received a small, gold caterpillar pin for her courage and bravery. Leslie L. Irvin founded The Caterpillar Club in 1922. The name of the club was chosen because a caterpillar lowers itself to earth by the silken thread it spins and the only people eligible to join the club are those whose lives have been saved by baling out of an aircraft in flight, using a parachute to reach the ground.

Courage and a great deal of love, was what bound Guy Lockhart and Judy Potter together.

Shortly after the wedding and with war looming, Guy was able to re-enlist with the RAFVR as a Sergeant Pilot flying Miles Master trainers and Spitfires. His son, Sauvan, was born in March 1940. In June 1941, Guy was posted to 602 Squadron flying Spitfires. Later the same month, he was transferred to 74 Squadron.

At this time the RAF took the offensive in a tactic which was designed to take the initiative away from the Luftwaffe. In March, Douglas Bader had taken over the Tangmere Wing, and he led the squadrons in the Circus Operations, which were large fighter sweeps escorting bombers at three different levels over German occupied France. This controversial brainchild of Douglas Bader resulted in many successes, but there was a high death toll and many aircraft were lost.

On the afternoon of 7th July 1941, Guy took off from Biggin Hill flying Spitfire W3317 in a Circus Operation. He was shot down by an enemy fighter near Ergny. Guy jumped out at about 16000 feet, and was knocked out when he hit a tree. His aeroplane came down a long distance away. Once Guy regained consciousness he found that he had injured an arm and a leg. He approached a farmer who refused to help him. The next person Guy met was a boy who told him that the farmer had telephoned the Germans in an attempt to claim the monetary reward that was on offer for information leading to the arrest of any evader. Fortunately, Guy was taken to safety at the house of Norbert Fillerin, who lived nearby in Renty. Together with his wife and three teenage children, he helped a number of evaders. Norbert was a calm, intelligent man, who was an active member of the escape line; he and the family took care of Guy until he was fit to continue his journey.

Alex Nitelet was shot down in the same area on 9th August, and was taken to the house of Vincent Ansel, a member of Norbert Filleren's organisation. Both of these airmen were among the very few who, like John Mott, came back twice to fight again.

On 10th August, Guy was on his way back. He was escorted via Lille, and here he joined Flying Officer Forde, whose Spitfire had been shot down on 23rd July over the Pas-de-Calais. The two men were taken to Abbeville where the Abbé Carpentier prepared false papers for them. They took a train to Paris, and then to Chalon across the demarcation line. When they left the train, Forde and the guide walked past the German guards but Guy was arrested. Fortunately, he spoke French convincingly, and held his own throughout four hours of interrogation through an interpreter. When this came to an end, he was escorted back to the railway station and ordered back to Paris.

Guy waited until dark, then boarded a goods train travelling in the opposite direction and made his way to Marseille. Guy stayed in Louis Nouveau's fifth floor apartment and together with his wife, Louis Nouveau sheltered over 150 escapers and evaders. Guy Lockhart is mentioned in his records as being the twenty fifth visitor there. The evening before Guy and a few others left the apartment, they were given instructions to shave before retiring for the night. Everyone needed to be dressed and ready by the time breakfast was served at 05:00 so that they could be at the station an hour later. Guy preferred to shave in the morning but, in his haste, he cut his face badly. Louis was cross with him, but had a remedy for bleeding razor cuts to hand, and it only caused a few minutes delay. As they left, Louis Nouveau asked them to look out for his son, 'Peter Bedard', if they were unfortunate enough to end up in the Miranda del Ebro concentration camp in Spain (Jean-Pierre Nouveau was travelling on French Canadian papers in that name). From the station, Guy was in a party that travelled to Pergnan, where they were handed over to a Spanish guide, who took them across the Pyrénées. Unfortunately, on arrival in Spain, they were indeed arrested and sent to Miranda del Ebro. Guy was the RAF lightweight boxing champion, and Louis Nouveau's son Jean-Pierre saw him box to entertain the captive troops. Like many other escapers and evaders who ended up here, a number of weeks passed before Guy was released for repatriation. He was flown home to RAF Mount Batten from Gibraltar on 21st October 1941. Like his wife, he was now entitled to wear the Caterpillar Club pin.

JOHN MOTT WAS ALSO A RECIPIENT OF THE PIN.
THE RUBY EYES INDICATE THAT THE AEROPLANE WAS ON FIRE WHEN HE PARACHUTED TO SAFETY – COURTESY OF KRISTINA O'BRIEN.

PART OF "MCCAIRNS J A (FLIGHT LIEUTENANT)" (PHOTOGRAPHS)
COURTESY IWM

The following month, on 26th November, he was posted to 138 Squadron as Pilot Officer (on probation), and in February 1942 he transferred to the new 161 Special

Duties Squadron, flying the Westland Lysander. John Mott also transferred from 138 to the Lysander flight with 161, and this is where the two men spent the next few months. Both of them enjoyed a game of bridge, and during the moon periods at Tangmere, it was an enjoyable way to pass the hours while waiting for the next mission. The Operations room at the cottage doubled up as a comfortable sitting room with plenty of chairs that could be drawn close to the cosy fire. There have been various descriptions of Guy over the years – the word eccentric has been used many times, and there have been a number of references to his meticulously neat appearance. In his off duty time, he enjoyed gambling in the London clubs, and, as Omar Sharif explained, many years later, 'playing bridge sharpens the mind for remembering the turn of the cards, no matter what other card game you play'. Undoubtedly, Guy's colleagues, including John, recognised first and foremost his skills as a pilot and his leadership qualities and John certainly valued his friendship.

Guy's first operational flight in Lysander V9428 took place on 1st March. Once he found the target, he was only on the ground for two minutes before bringing his passengers safely back to base.

On 20th March, Guy's two year old son, Sauvan, died as a result of contracting meningitis. In spite of this overwhelming personal tragedy, Guy was operational out of Tangmere within a week.

On 26th March, Guy took off from Tangmere in Lysander V9367 on an SOE Operation, BACCARAT II; his outbound passenger was BCRA agent Gilbert Renault-Roulier, aka Rémy, who was the head of the Confrérie Notre-Dame Intelligence Network. There was heavy cloud that made navigation difficult until the River Loire became visible and gave Guy the chance get back on track. The target was a field called the Roi de Coeur, which was situated near St Leger de Montbrillais, in the Deux-Sèvres. When he applied the brakes upon landing, the Lysander became bogged down in a ploughed area of the field. The rear axle became caught in mud and grass, and the engine power proved to be insufficient. Rémy went for help, the reception party used their combined manpower to pull the Lysander round, and Guy was able to manoeuvre it onto firm ground. Seventeen minutes after landing, he was airborne with two passengers; Christian Pineau, aka Garnier of the Libération Nord, and Colonel François Faure, aka Pako, who was an assistant to Rémy. The clouds cleared just as they reached the English coast, and they landed safely at Tangmere at 01:45. The two Frenchmen were taken to Bignor Manor to sleep before being taken to London.

This visit by Christian Pineau was of major significance. His meeting with Charles de Gaulle was a difficult one, but he ensured that the General was in no doubt about the significance of the Resistance movement, and the huge risks the members took with their own lives and those of their families. On 23rd June, the clandestine papers in France published a major declaration by General de Gaulle.

Many years later a wooden memorial was unveiled by the side of the road, near the landing site, commemorating this operation. Guy's daughter Tanya was present at the invitation of Christian Pineau.

The wooden memorial has now been replaced by one made of polished stone with an RAF roundel at the top. The text reads:

Saint leger de Montbrillas site de la resistance. Reseau CND
Terrain Homologue: 'Roi De Coeur' nuit 26/27 Mars 1942
un avion 'LYSANDER' pilote par GUY LOCKHART Debarque de Londres
'Gilbert Renault' alias 'Remy' sont repatis
'Francois Faure' alias 'Paco'
'Christian Pineau' alias 'Garnier'
en mission pour la liberation de la France.

Amongst his other activities during the month he spent in England, Christian Pineau underwent training in radio messages and in the choice of sites for landings and parachute drops. Before he left, he agreed to work with the Free French Intelligence and to set up intelligence circuits in each zone. He returned to France by Lysander, during the next moon period, on the night of 27th April.

Between the March and April moon periods, Squadron 161 moved from Graveley to Tempsford, near the village of Sandy in Bedfordshire. This became the permanent home for the two special duties squadrons.

Towards the end of April, Guy had a particularly difficult landing on Faucon Field, 10 miles NNE of Chateauroux. The landing strip was on a hill. This resulted in a dramatic landing, leading to an engine fire, and it was only with great difficulty that Guy was able to continue. His passengers were Gaston Tavian (Collin) and Lt de Vaisseau Mariotti (Rousseau). Tavian had chosen the unsuitable site and as a result of this near disaster, the Air Ministry ruled that in future all fields would be chosen by agents trained in England, or by the pilots themselves. Tavian was duly trained before his return to France.

Back in Tangmere, on 28th May 1942, Guy was preparing for SOE Operation GEAN. John Mott, who was flying the same night, was due to deliver Alex Nitelet, as a much needed wireless operator, sent by Jimmy Langley to the PAT Line. The three evaders had no notion that before long they would each join the ranks of the very few airmen who came back twice to fight again.

At this time it was normal procedure for the Lysander pilots and their passengers to have dinner together in the cottage at Tangmere. It was here that the pilots briefed their passengers on how to operate the sliding roof of the rear cockpit, how and when they could use the intercom, and the fact that on landing they were required to pass out all their luggage and stow the luggage for the inbound passengers, before climbing out of the aeroplane via the fixed ladder. This particular evening must have been unique; the three men were strictly forbidden to discuss any details about themselves or how they came to be there.

Had an unrestricted conversation been possible, Guy and Alex could have shared the mutual experience of being shot down and injured in a Spitfire on a Circus Operation, just one month apart. They were both sheltered and assisted by Norbert Filleren and his organisation; Guy's journey home commenced just one day after Alex arrived in Renty. John and Alex had met during the evenings of their debriefing days in London, immediately after Christmas, when they were each in discussions with the newly formed IS9. However, all three of them were totally aware of the regulations that forbade any such conversations. The brief friendship between Alex and John was to be of significant importance when they met again later in the war.

Guy took off from Tangmere in Lysander V9597 at 23:25. He was carrying one passenger and 150lbs of baggage, and he was due to land in a field north of Chateauroux, near Les Vignots. The weather deteriorated as he approached his target area. He received no return signal from either the landing field, or the two alternate fields. After circling for an hour, he returned to Tangmere, landing at 05:20. André Simon had requested this pick up after his failed negotiations to exfiltrate the ex-Prime Minister of France Edouard Delaldier. André had been arrested some hours earlier.

John Mott took off on the same night on Operation TENTATIVE. He landed his Lysander V9595 near Issoudun to deliver his friend, Alex Nitelet, who had now trained as a radio operator for the PAT escape line. John's Lysander had become bogged down on landing, and although Alex was delivered safely, John was arrested. He was sent to La Châtre barracks at Châteauroux, where he joined André Simon. On 2nd June, Guy completed the entries for May, in John's logbook and signed it on John's behalf.

The escape lines were in a chaotic state at this time, and the pickup operations were suspended for a while. Guy was tasked with flying bombing missions to Normandy during this time. The London Gazette, dated 5th June, listed the award of the Distinguished Flying Cross; this award came with the citation:

'This officer recently completed 3 operations, involving much preparation and difficult organisation. Flight Lieutenant Lockhart worked hard to achieve success and surmounted many difficulties with great skill and initiative.'

Pick-up operations resumed during the August moon period. Guy was, by now, Acting Squadron Leader, having received rapid promotion, owing to his undoubted skills as a pilot and as an inspirational leader. He successfully completed Operation MERCURY on 23rd August.

On 31st August, Guy took off from Tangmere in Lysander V9597, at 21:50, on Operation BOREAS II. He landed on his target field, but crashed into a grass-covered ditch, and, in spite of the Lysander's robust structure, the undercarriage was destroyed. The ground party were entirely culpable for this unforgiveable error.

Gérard Gauthier wrote of this incident, recalling what his parents had told him. His father had been one of the reception committee. The secret landing ground in the Saône valley was code-named Faison. M Gauthier was put in charge of the security of the outbound luggage, while the pilot and passengers discussed the situation some way off. The agent who had laid out the flare path was caught attempting to open one of the suitcases. When he was challenged, the group came back to sort him out. The passengers awaiting their flight to Tangmere were Christian Pineau and Jean Cavailles. Pineau was so angry that he announced that the man should be executed immediately, but he didn't carry this threat through. Recalling the episode, Pineau later wrote that Tarn, the trained agent, had not complied with the safety distances, intending to cause an accident. He knew that the mail intended for London contained a very unfavourable report on his behaviour, so he had sabotaged the operation, to prevent this report from reaching its destination.

Guy destroyed the IFF (Identification Friend/Foe radar impulse) and ensured that his inbound passenger escaped with the reception committee. Having agreed a rendez-vous, he waited an hour before setting fire to the Lysander, and in the meantime he destroyed the auxiliary petrol tank with an axe. When he set fire to the aircraft, it burned for two hours, and was completely destroyed.

When they met up, they all walked together along the railway line, and spent one night with the Gauthier family. Finding trousers for Guy presented a problem: M. Gauthier was five feet nine inches tall, and, as his RAF records show, Guy was three and a half inches taller, so the trousers provided for him flapped round his ankles.

Mme. Gauthier later cut up Guy's coat to make a coat for her oldest son. She kept the uniform buttons in her button box, and carefully stored Guy's silk maps, which were eventually inherited by her daughter.

The following day, Guy was taken to Lyon, where he was sheltered by Yves Farge, the editor of the Progrès de Lyon. Yves kitted him out with blue, railway workman's overalls, before he was taken to Narbonne Plage. Arrangements had been made to evacuate Guy and his passengers by sea to Gibraltar, in the planned Operation LEDA, on the night of 5th September. This was an SIS/BCRA operation by the Polish crewed felucca, Seadog, which was captained by Lt Jan Buchowski. Unfortunately, two coast-guards arrived before the men being picked up could board the vessel and chaos ensued. Some shots were fired, but Guy managed to swim out to the Seadog. Christian Pineau was caught and imprisoned on a black market charge, but he managed to escape and continue his work with the Resistance until he was arrested again in 1943. Guy returned to the UK in a 138 S D aeroplane on 13th September.

On 13th July, the SOE agent, André Simon, who failed to show for Guy's pick-up on 28th May, had been brought out on Operation LUCILE from St Pierre Plage, near Narbonne. This was for the SIS (MI9) Operation BLUEBOTTLE.

The London Gazette, dated 9th October 1942 listed the award of the Distinguished Service Order. This award came with the citation:

> 'Squadron Leader Lockhart has participated in many operational sorties, and the successes gained can be attributed largely to his careful organisation and planning. He has, at all times, displayed courage, skill and fortitude, which have been in keeping with the highest traditions of the Royal Air Force.'

When Guy continued to fly the Lysander operations, he became known as Wing Commander Henri; this was an essential ruse so that he could not be identified if he was downed again. In January 1943 he was transferred to the Air Ministry to work in AI2c. This department had operational responsibility for Special Duties flights into North West Europe. Little is known of Guy's activities during the next ten months other than his involvement with the need to land aircraft in Poland to pick-up couriers who had been parachuted in. Their journeys were taking months, and many of them went missing. The proposed operation was code-named 'WILDHORN'. Now, with the rank of Acting Wing Commander, Guy considered that a Hudson could be used for this work if the range could be extended by the use of extra fuel tanks. Until this point in time, all such operations took place during the moon periods, but the concern about the effects that the weather might have if there was an undue delay, led to a mission being carried out during the non-moon period. The first operation went ahead successfully, owing to the Polish pilots' uniquely thorough knowledge of the terrain. Other Special Duties Operations during these non-moon periods only began to take place at a later date, with the use of the 'Rebecca'/'Eureka' system, which became standard practice, in due course.

In November 1943, 627 Squadron was formed at Oakington, in Cambridgeshire, as a Mosquito light-bomber unit flying with No. 8 Group Pathfinder Force. Guy joined the squadron as the Flight Commander. He transferred to 692 Squadron when it was formed at the beginning of January 1944 at Graveley, in Huntingdonshire. During his time with this squadron, Guy famously lost an engine on his way to bomb Berlin, but he completed the operation and returned safely to base. The Pathfinders were the first to arrive over a target; they identified it and marked it with flares so that the main force of bombers could pinpoint their aim. The Pathfinder crews were entitled to wear the distinctive eagle badge on their uniform pocket flap, but not when they were on an operation because it would mark them out as elite crews, if they were captured.

Following the loss of the Commanding Officer of No. 7 Squadron, Air Vice-Marshall Don Bennet asked Guy to transfer as the new C/O. He was posted to his new command on 1st January, and was now flying Lancaster bombers. He was flying on his fourth operation with the squadron when he lost his life.

At 22:26 on the night of 27th April, he took off from RAF Oakington, in a Lancaster Mk III, JB676 for a bombing raid on Freidrichschafen. The primary targets at Freidrichschafen were the Zeppelin hangers, which were being used for the production of tank gearboxes and aircraft radios. Guy's aircraft was shot down by a night fighter, and crashed at Reichenbach near Lahr/Schwaszwald. The entire crew of seven died in the crash.

Guy Lockhart is buried in Durnbach Cemetery, Germany.

In his autobiography, Don Bennett wrote of Guy: 'I never, throughout the entire war, met anybody so fanatically courageous and 'press-on' at all times and in all circumstances. Virtually nothing would stop him…his determination passed all bounds.'

The London Gazette dated 6th June 1944 listed the award of the Distinguished Flying Cross; this award came with the citation:

'In February, 1944, this officer was posted to form and command No. 692 Squadron. Since then he has shown outstanding ability, and his leadership has been largely responsible for the fine record set up by the squadron. Wing Commander Lockhart has also continued to operate against the enemy with unremitting keenness and zeal, and has taken part in many operational sorties with success.'

In addition, Guy Lockhart was awarded the Croix de Guerre.[4]

---

4 In a death notice placed by Elizabeth Potter, his widow's sister, Guy's awards include the Czechoslovakian Flying Cross. Grateful Czechoslovakian units often presented RAF pilots with their own wings, these were worn on the opposite side to the RAF wings. It seems likely that this is what Hugh Verity mistook for the French military wings that he mentions in his description of Guy, whose son, Sauvan, was named after a brave Czechoslovakian pilot.

9

THE FORT DU LA DUCHÈRE AND CHAMBARAN CAMP

Moving the eight officers to the Fort de la Duchère was a temporary measure, brought on by the anger of the Italian commission, because of escapes from the Fort de la Revère. Detachment W had been in existence for nearly two years, and the officers and other ranks had been accommodated separately. However, there were communication channels open throughout, and the officers had been able to create opportunities for escapes. The French military were determined to change this by keeping the officers entirely separate from the other ranks.

Camp du Chambaran, Isère, had formally been a French Air Force training camp, in the foothills of the Alps, near Grenoble. There were plenty of barrack huts where the other ranks could be accommodated, and new accommodation was being built in a separate area. The building had not been completed when the decision was made to close the Fort de la Revère. The officers and orderlies were transported to Lyon, which was just inside the German Zone. The Fort de la Duchère was a five sided fort to the north west of the city. Three new arrivals joined them during the first few days of September. These officers had been in the thick of the carnage at Dieppe on 19th August. Operation JUBILEE had been a hard fought battle against unexpectedly strong defences. At the fort, the new Senior British Officer was now Lieutenant

Commander Redvers Prior DSC RN. At Dieppe, when the ammunition ran out while fighting a rearguard action to cover the retreat of the survivors on the beach, he had eventually been forced to surrender. He had been injured several times during action and was put onto a hospital train. In spite of his injuries, he escaped from the train and spent weeks behind enemy lines before he was recaptured. During those weeks, he had come across the West Wall, which was an enormous fortification the Germans were building in case of an invasion. He also came across installations for V weapons. In spite of being in a poor physical and mental state, he was now determined to find a way to escape and bring back all the information he had gleaned, as well as the lessons that should be learned from the Dieppe raid.

John was completely unaware that his brother, Mervyn, had been incredibly lucky to survive the action at Dieppe. Mervyn was serving on HMS Albrighton, which was a hunt-class destroyer of the Royal Navy, based in Portsmouth. By the time of the Dieppe Raid, the Albrighton had escorted more than 300 convoys in the English Channel. At Dieppe, together with her sister ship HMS Berkeley and others, her guns provided cover for the landing parties and bombarded the shore batteries.

Decades later, Mervyn wrote:

'Most of the time we were engaged in protective Coastal Convoy duty, through the English Channel, but we occasionally took part in offensive patrols against enemy shipping.

My post at sea was as a Bridge lookout, where I could observe all that was going on, but when we went to Action Stations, I was in the Transmitting Station, an enclosed area behind the Bridge in which the machinery for controlling the main armament was installed. While we were in there we were completely cut off from the outside world, except for a telephone.

In August 1942, we took part in some exercises off the Dorset Coast which turned out to be a practice for the Dieppe Raid, although we were not aware of this until we sailed for the French Coast.

During the raid itself, the ship was hit by at least three shells. We suffered casualties and extensive damage, but were able to pick up survivors from our sister ship HMS Berkeley, which was badly damaged by a bomb. I spent most of the action in the Transmitting Station, but I was then sent on deck to help pick up the survivors, and saw the launch of the torpedoes, which we used to scuttle HMS Berkeley after her crew had been removed. I was isolated in the Transmitting Station with five others for the remainder of the battle.

On return to Portsmouth, we had to land the survivors, and then land all our remaining ammunition before we could dock the ship. It was then that I learned that a shell had passed right through the ship without exploding, a few feet below where I had been sitting.'

The discipline at the Fort de la Duchère was much stricter than at the Fort de la Revère. Exercise was only allowed at prescribed times, and the men were made to feel that they were prisoners at every turn. Personal correspondence was subjected to severe censorship, but the food was the same as was served to the French officers, and there were plenty of Red Cross parcels.

The conversion of the camp that was taking place at Chambaran was comprehensive, with massive amounts of barbed wire along the illuminated perimeter, and the addition of a watchtower at each corner. The guard in each watchtower had a machine gun and control of a powerful searchlight. Further barbed wire barriers were installed to separate the men's accommodation from that being built for the officers. In the meantime, General Mer, who was Chief of the 14th Military Division in Lyons, decided that he wished to prohibit the POWs from wearing civvies. Most of the men still had civilian clothes, as well as the uniforms that had been supplied to them at the Fort de la Revère. Consequently, appropriate uniforms were supplied for each man. The internees had until now been able to keep abreast of news from home on their radios, but these were now banned by the authorities.

The Commandant at Chambaran was Chef de Bataillon Bouvetier, who reported to the Military Chief of the Isère region, Colonel Georges Malraison, based in Grenoble. These two did their very best to improve the quality of life for their prisoners and in order that the men could still be informed, they arranged for a radio situated in the guards' quarters to blare out the English language BBC news.

Many in the French military were disgusted at the failure in political and military leadership since the beginning of the war, and they were not prepared to follow the elderly Marshall Petain without questioning his judgement, in spite of his brilliant record in WW1. Immediately after the armistice, Colonel Malraison, who at that time was stationed at Brax, told his junior officers that they would be provisionally demobilized in a few days, but he wished to remind them of their duty while he was still their Commander. He told them to be ready for revenge so that when the new army came into being, no matter how small, it would be prepared for its vital role in the future. Not long after this, the army had been reduced right down until it had become the token l'Armée de l'Armistice.

The remaining men from the Fort de la Revère had arrived in mid September. There were just eleven officers and four orderlies at the Fort de la Duchère, at the beginning of October, and because one of the orderlies had managed to escape, they were all moved to Chambaran, which was a journey of about thirty five miles.

The Rev. Donald Caskie was permitted to conduct Protestant services once a month. This journey was now a simple one as he was based in Grenoble. On one visit the Commandant expressed his concern about the severe depression affecting Redvers Prior, and at the end of the meeting between the two men, Donald Caskie promised that he would do all he could to help Redvers Prior, if he could escape and make his way to the hotel in Grenoble where Donald Caskie was living. John had developed a good relationship with the Commandant and, with his knowledge of French, was always willing to speak on behalf of any of the others. It must have been difficult for all concerned to cope with the intense anxiety, which was affecting the SBO Lieutenant Commander Prior at that time.

There were a number of new arrivals at Chambaran, including some SOE agents, and more survivors of the Dieppe raid. Amongst these arrivals was a man listed as J Nitey. This was John's friend Alex Nitelet, who never revealed his true identity, but John vouched for him as a pilot he had known earlier in the war.

During the latter part of October, the battle of El Alamein began, with John's brother Pip in the thick of it. One week into November, Operation TORCH brought the coastline of French North Africa under Allied control. The German High Command responded by ordering the occupation of the whole of France, in spite of the Armistice treaties. From 11th November, the Italians took over the area to the East of the Rhône, and the Germans took over the rest. Commandant Bouvetier immediately tried to find a way to free all his prisoners, but Colonel Malraison stopped this notion in its tracks. However, Commandant Bouvetier had already made some phone calls, and he was removed from his post the following morning, and subsequently dismissed from the army. He was replaced by Chef de Bataillon Tournier. John took it on himself to plead the case of Alex Nitelet, and various other approaches were made on behalf of those involved at Dieppe and the other SOE agents. Colonel Malraison considered the various requests and decided to act on his own authority, knowing that passing a request any higher would produce a negative result. He was aware of dossiers that made it quite obvious that the men named would be dealt with in the harshest manner if the Germans got hold of them. With help from the team immediately around him, he compiled a list of ten names, and decided to permit the escape of these specific prisoners. Each of these men was summoned to the camp office where the details of the plan were explained. It is a matter of record that only nine men were released, and various writers over the decades have guessed at the identity of the tenth man. However, every guess has been wide of the mark; John Mott must have been devastated when he was told that there was a dossier on him, listing his activities assisting the resistance during his evasion, and warning him that he must avoid falling into the hands of the Germans at all costs. He immediately knew from this that his beloved friends and colleagues had been betrayed, and he certainly was not going to give any credence to what he was being told. Somehow he laughed it off and told the Commandant that they must be writing about someone else.

The nine men who had been assisted in their escape all returned safely to England, and even those who travelled in the company of Alex Nitelet remained unaware of his part in connecting them up with the PAT escape line, such was his ability to remain anonymous.

At the end of November, Hitler ordered the dissolution of the armistice army, and a few days later Italian soldiers arrived at Chambaran Camp with a fleet of buses and ambulances. They gave the prisoners just thirty minutes to pack up and leave for Italy. Some of the mail from this camp only travelled as far as Paris, where it was found and distributed towards the end of the war. John's letters home are postmarked Sutton, May 1945.

10

FROM GAVI TO ESCAPE

On 6th December, a large company of Italian soldiers accompanied the men on their journey towards the Italian frontier. At Modane, the prisoners were split up, and the officers were escorted on the train to Campo 5 at Gavi, which lies in Allesandria, twenty miles northwest of Genoa. Gavi housed up to two hundred inmates defined as 'Ufficiale percolosi e turbéulenti' (dangerous or turbulent). The majority were from the Army, but there was also a substantial number from the Navy and the RAF.

On arrival at Gavi, the prisoners found themselves in a large, attractive village. Their luggage was left in a pile in the market place, and they climbed 600 feet, on a steep zigzag path up a hill, to the imposing black fortress at the top. The utterly impregnable fortress had been built in the fourteenth century as part of a ring of defences protecting the Genoese Republic. Over the ensuing centuries, it became famed for the fact that it had never been taken by assault, and there had been no escapes.

Campo 5 at Gavi was opened in June 1941, and the experience of arriving here was to be repeated many times, as the number of inmates increased between then and September 1943. The black masonry walls towered above the forbidding black hole that was the tunnelled entrance. The passage was dank, dark and foul-smelling, and there were rough, stone steps leading down to massive iron-faced doors. Behind the doors was a long tunnel lined with guardrooms, a huge metal grille at the end, opening onto the lower courtyard, which housed the other ranks in dark, windowless rooms, each housing ten men, the kitchen with the Officers' Mess above it, and rooms at the top for some of the officers. John was housed on this floor.

Leading up to another courtyard there was a steep, narrow ramp with a brick floor, which wound its way round the edge of the rock and through a tunnel. On the rock side there were very damp rooms, which housed the more junior officers, and the later arrivals, eight to a room. On the open cliff side of the courtyard there was a newer building, overlooking the village of Gavi that housed the rest of the officers. One of the few ways to keep fit was to walk down and run up the steep path separating the two courtyards. Prior to the arrival of the POWs, the fortress had been used as a civil gaol for criminals; it is thought that its use for that purpose had been discontinued, because it proved too damp and unhealthy in the winter. There were insufficient latrines and a permanent shortage of water.

Later events seemed to prove that the prisoners arriving with John did not undergo the detailed search imposed upon others, on arrival in Campo 5, as some of them managed to retain various small items for use in future escape attempts.

Hundreds of guards lived in overcrowded huts on a lower terrace outside the walls of the fortress. The Camp Commandant was Colonel Moscatelli. He had an imposing physique and kept rigid control over all aspects of the prison. Known as 'Joe Grapes', the Commandant was intensely disliked by the prisoners, and he doled out punishments at the slightest excuse. His officers were to be seen and felt at all hours, constantly checking on every activity of the prisoners. They had large spy-holes in the cell doors so that they could watch the prisoners day and night. Early that year, the basic food rations in Italian camps had been cut drastically, owing to the poverty of the surrounding country. The prisoners now found themselves confined and living in very difficult circumstances. Now and then, a walk was organised for about twelve prisoners under heavy guard, up to a bridge. There they rested for ten minutes, and then retraced their steps, but they were always within sight of the guards on the prison walls. Each prisoner averaged about one walk a month.

A delegation from the Swiss protecting power tried to get the conditions improved, but not many changes took place, other than the provision of a dentist.

When John arrived, it was approaching mid-winter, and fresh foods were difficult to source locally. A detail of guards went down to the village every morning and brought back whatever fresh vegetables were available. The Mess took what they needed from the Red Cross parcels and cooked the best meals they could muster. The Senior British Officer (SBO) was a New Zealander called Lieutenant Colonel Ken Fraser, and by all accounts he did an excellent job. Together with a hand picked team, he gained the willing cooperation of all the men. Ken Fraser was the former CO of the 5th New Zealand Field Regiment and was universally admired for his skill and tact in controlling unruly prisoners, and dealing with the captors.

James Moore Ratcliffe, or 'Ratty', was the highly respected Adjutant who was later to play a vital role in John's journey home. Ratcliffe trained as an engineer and had worked for six years as a statistician with Morris Motors before he joined The Middlesex Regiment and then via No 7 Commando had to come to serve with the Special Boat Service. He led a team of four in two folbots (folding kayaks), scouting the Libyan coast, as part of the abortive scheme to capture Rommel. Unfortunately the submarine involved failed to make the agreed rendezvous, so they had to head off on foot in two teams to try to reach the Allied lines. Together with Trevor Ravenscroft, Ratcliffe walked two hundred miles across the mountainous Jebel desert, near Tobruk. The journey took eleven days without food and four days without water, only for them to be captured by the Italians and sent to Gavi.

The following March another New Zealander, Brigadier George Clifton, arrived and took over as the SBO. He was a fearless and dashing character, and was happy to leave the current team in place under him. This was made particularly easy by the existing friendship between him and Ken Fraser. The hardness of life at Gavi and this excellent leadership led to a deep bond between the officers that had been thrown together in this dreadful place.

There was no grass inside the fortress walls and nowhere to sit. However, the prisoners were able to purchase locally made wicker chairs, and they carried these as they went from place to place. They also each kept a cardboard Red Cross box, containing personal tins of condensed milk, sugar and jam, etc., plus cutlery, plates and a mug. Breakfast was served every day and the men sat around scrubbed tables, each of which could seat six. Stewed prunes or pasta porridge were the norm, but at least it was a breakfast and made a good start to the day. Roll call was at eight, and after that the Italians unlocked the iron grilles that separated the two levels. The batmen then arrived with just enough hot water for shaving. The men shaved desert style with a mug of hot water in one hand and their shaving brush or razor in the other hand.

The POWs who had fought in the desert were no strangers to water shortage. One of these, who was to play a part in John's escape, was Allan Yeoman of the Second New Zealand Expeditionary Force. Before his capture, he had played a vital role in the beginning of the First Battle of El Alamein, as it came to be known, at Ruweisat Ridge. John was completely unaware that his younger brother Pip was deeply embroiled in the same battle.

Allan Yeoman was with his brigade at the time General Auchinleck took personal command of the Eighth Army, and decided to make a stand on a line running from El Alamein to the Qattara Depression — the now famous Alamein Line. On 14th July 1942 the first of a series of actions in the First Battle of El Alamein began when General Rommel launched his initial attacks on the final Allied defensive line before the Nile. Although these initial attacks were thwarted, the German and Italian forces continued to grow in strength.

To forestall any further attacks, General Auchinleck ordered immediate counter-attacks with whatever forces were at hand. With elements from the 2nd New Zealand Division, the attack was to clear the enemy from the positions along the Ruweisat Ridge that commanded the middle of the Allied line. The New Zealand brigades captured the western end of Ruweisat Ridge, but the British 22nd Armoured Brigade did not arrive as planned. Lacking tank support, or effective anti-tank defences, the New Zealanders were assailed by waves of German tanks, and finally overrun that evening. At the eastern end of Ruweisat Ridge, the Indian 5th Infantry Brigade took its objectives by mid afternoon, with the help of the British 2nd Armoured Brigade. They then moved west along Ruweisat Ridge, arriving at the New Zealand positions, and pushing the panzers off the ridge.

Ruweisat Ridge was important because, although it rose only about twenty feet above the surrounding desert, and was hardly discernible at any distance, it was actually 200 feet above sea level, and dominated over a hundred square miles.

Pip Mott, one of John's two brothers, was a major with the Indian 5th Infantry Brigade, and many years after the war he wrote:

'Over the years I have heard people say "When we stood alone…" but we never did stand alone and certainly not at Alamein. There was a Greek Brigade to the south, plus French legionnaires of the Foreign Legion (not Frenchmen in the kepi but French Colonial troops wearing the fez) and there were Rhodesian

Anti-Tank gunners; there were South Africans, Indians, New Zealanders and Australians and no doubt others who do not come to mind at this moment. With the Germans and the Italians on the other side it was more a case of the world at war, than anyone standing alone.'

Another prisoner at Gavi, who was to play an important role in John's escape, was Captain Robert Frederick Parrott of the 31st Field Regiment Royal Artillery (4th Indian Division). He had been captured at Halfaya Pass and imprisoned in Camp 41 at Montalbo. After a betrayed escape attempt he was sent to Gavi and was determined to try to escape again.

When the New Zealander Captain Daniel Riddiford, was confined to a prison cell on his arrival at Gavi, he found that the worst thing to cope with was the dank cold; the only possibility of getting warm was to tuck up in bed. Food was fine as it was delivered from the Mess kitchen and the best was always sent to the cells. He was allowed one hour of exercise after breakfast.

Walking up and down the upper courtyard, he found two other prisoners there pacing up and down. One of them was Parrott who told him that there were always a few of the inmates 'inside'; on this occasion he was there for insulting one of the guards.

He told Riddiford that there was a first class crowd of chaps at Gavi, mostly there because they had all previously attempted to escape or because they were captured commandos. He explained that he had earlier been in the cell that Riddiford was now occupying, and asked him not to try tunnelling through the back wall, as that had already been achieved, providing access to a walled up passage, behind which Parrott had been able to walk the whole length of the cells, but that was as far as they he had managed to reach. Tunnels in the nearby cells had also been dug so that the prisoners could go through them into the passage at the back and visit each other. He hoped to have another shot at it in the spring, but in the meantime it had been sealed up.

The same afternoon, the two of them met again, in their permitted exercise hour, after lunch. Parrott briefed Riddiford to be careful not to let any officer see them talking, and to be sure to stand at attention if the Commandant appeared. Almost immediately, the tall, elderly and immaculate Colonel Giuseppe Moscatelli arrived with his entourage. In all the ex-prisoners' accounts about their sojourn in Campo Five, there is not one good word written about this man.

John and some of his fellow officers discovered that their rooms were above the disused wine cellars, and it was possible to gain access to these from the solitary confinement cells which were situated alongside their rooms. Thus the plans were hatched to tunnel a way out from one of these cellars. Joe Grapes was quick to punish any perceived misdemeanour, so it was easy for those involved in the scheme to bait the guards in order to spend time in solitary confinement, and carry on with the task in turn.

The escape committee was kept very busy investigating the various escape plans hatched by the prisoners. There was always plenty of hope and hard work going on, and the occasional break for freedom. Noisy games of volleyball were constantly played to cover up the sound of tunnelling. Masking the sound of such activities was a speciality of one particularly skilled individual; Norman Blair was an RAF ground gunner who had been on airfield defence duties when he was captured. He acquired a piano accordion that had been donated by the Red Cross and took on the task of arranging concerts, where he accompanied noisy participants singing loudly with lots of foot stamping, keeping time with the music.

Tommy Macpherson had been commissioned in the Queen's Own Cameron Highlanders Territorial Army in 1939, and then served in No.11 Scottish Commando. Part of the same abortive folbot mission, he was captured one day after Jim Ratcliffe and Trevor Ravenscroft, as he and Corporal Evans tried to make it overland to Tobruck. He ended up at Gavi after a failed attempt to escape from the POW camp at Montalbo. Determined to escape again, he devoted his time to perfecting his knowledge of Italian. Two Italian newspapers were made available each day, so Macpherson studied them carefully for useful news, and then over dinner in the Mess he proceeded to pass on what he had gleaned from the highly prejudiced accounts he had read.

On a daily basis, a radio amplifier also blared out the daily news in Italian across the compound.

Much of the mail destined for the Italian camps was lost or destroyed by the Italian censors, probably through laziness on their part. The inefficiency of the Italian administration handicapped communications to such an extent that code messages and escape equipment often took more than a year to reach the camps.

Other than his close friendship with Micky Carmichael, typically the only thing John spoke of with regard to Gavi after the war centred on the fable of Princess Gavia, the daughter of Clodimir, who was King of the Franks.

The story goes that Gavia had fallen in love with a handsome young man who served as a guard in her father's court. The two of them sought the King's permission to marry, but he refused to have his daughter wed out of her class. Desperate to be together, they eloped and fled to the other side of the Alps to a beautiful village, and there they built the fortress at the top of a hill. The King's troops searched the countryside in vain until the husband was in the village one day and, having drunk a little too much of the lovely local wine, told the innkeeper their story. The innkeeper kept the young man drinking and listened sympathetically, then sent him to bed, and sent word to the King to gain a handsome reward. The couple were collected by the King's troops and brought back home to face their punishment.

By this time, word of the romance had spread throughout the kingdom, and there were intercessions on Gavia's behalf by Alamasunta, Queen of the Goths, as well as by Pope St. Hermistas. The King, of course, upon looking into his lovely daughter's eyes, could not help but forgive her. He blessed their union, and as a wedding gift he bequeathed them the town in which they had chosen to settle. In her honour he gave the name Gavi to the town.

The most important fellow prisoner in John's subsequent escape was George Michael Carmichael (Micky). He was the son of a First World War hero, Group Captain Ivan Carmichael. In March 1915, Carmichael had destroyed the rails at Menin railway station by dropping a 100lb bomb from just 120 feet, having cut a hole under his feet in his aeroplane to ensure the accuracy of the drop. Micky and his brother, John William Carmichael, both joined the RAF. In November 1941, Micky was captured in the advance party, which was taking over the aerodrome at Gaz El Aarid. He escaped from a train, which was taking him from Taranto to Padua, was recaptured, and was sent to Gavi on 19th June 1943, where he struck up a friendship with John.

The baking summer of 1943 brought much news for the prisoners to absorb. They heard of the wonderful successes of the Eighth Army and of the landings in Sicily. The Italians became more and more dispirited, and the prisoners began serious keep fit regimes in preparation for what lay ahead. In June, there was a brief announcement that Mussolini had been dismissed, and Badoglio had assumed command of the state. Now it seemed obvious that Italy would soon surrender unconditionally, and the War Office sent coded instructions to all the SBOs in the Italian camps of the action they should take when this came to fruition. In the event of an Italian surrender, the prisoners were to stay in the camps until staff officers were flown in to arrange their orderly evacuation. These instructions were to gain long-term notoriety as the 'Stay Put' order. [5]

On receiving these instructions, Clifton decided to treat the communication as a dead letter, and continued to make other plans with his team.

Individuals had slowly but surely, made their own escape tools. Rubbing a table knife on the stone floor eventually squared the end to form a functioning screw driver; sharpening one knife on the floor, then cutting into the blade of a second one, enabled a prisoner to create a makeshift saw. In spite of many searches, some of the men had managed to retain the tips of their bayonets in the hope of being able to use them when an opportunity arose.

Once the Allies had gained a foothold in Southern Italy, it was no surprise to the prisoners who were situated in the north of the country to observe the arrival of some German troops in the village below. However, these men were part of the Veterinary Corps, with horse-drawn transport; they appeared to be well past their youth, and even in large numbers they did not seem to represent a significant threat.

News of the Armistice came during dinner on 9th September, when a shout went up from the Italian quarters, and lights started to appear in the village of Gavi, as the inhabitants tore the blackout curtains from their windows. Clifton went straight to the Commandant to demand immediate release of all the prisoners; this was refused on the grounds that it would be too dangerous while the camp was surrounded by Germans. After dinner, the officers climbed the ramp once more to be locked in by the Italians.

The following morning, an Italian ration party made the usual trip to the village to collect fresh supplies, and one of these guards made a playful gesture with his gun towards a German soldier, who promptly shot him. He was howling with pain, so his colleagues hastily gathered him up, and headed back into the fortress where he later died. The Germans had, by now, despatched front line infantry forces to secure the prisoners, and ordered the Veterinary Corps to take over the fortress. The Commandant was not on the premises, and once the fortress was surrounded, it took no time at

---

5 The head of MI9, Brigadier Norman Crockatt, instinctively disliked the prospect of mass breakouts. He believed that it would cause chaos on the battlefield, and might precipitate reprisals by parts of the Italian army, who did not support the surrender. Furthermore, he considered the malnourished POWs to be of little value as fighting soldiers.

He concluded that Monty would sweep up Italy in a matter of a few days anyway. All things considered, they believed that the best alternative was to tell the POWs to 'stay put' and wait in their camps for the Allied forces to arrive.

all for his elderly deputy to appear with ten men, and head down the slope towards the village waving a large white flag. Once again, Gavi had lived up to its centuries old history of surrendering, without firing a shot. Inside the fortress, the prisoners were in a frenzy of activity, as they now had information of the exact location of an ancient tunnel to the village. This tunnel had been the direct route into the centre of the village, created for Princess Gavia, so many years earlier. The German front line infantry moved in and took over from the Italians. This gave the prisoners some advantages as the newcomers were unaware which areas were normally out of bounds, thus enabling the prisoners to start work to try and clear the entrance to the tunnel. It was also possible for one of the friendly Italians to remove some of the records from the offices, and with great speed and determination, everything the prisoners could think of was done to confuse the situation. All kinds of escape plans were put into practise. Those who chose to stay and hide were ordered to log the particulars, and ensure that they stowed enough food and water.[6]

Another company of Germans arrived and took surrender of all the arms held by the Italians. By the Monday morning, most of the plans were complete, but at 09:00 the news went round that the Germans had given everyone in the camp just an hour's notice to be ready to move to Germany. Chaos ensued as the prisoners rushed around to hide or gather up their belongings to head off.

Bob Parrott, along with Major Eric Gibbon, Captain Tony Hay and Captain Griffiths, had chosen to hide under a slab-tiled roof above a passage outside Room 14; they had stashed enough food for two weeks though they didn't expect to hide for that long.

The bulk of the prisoners were gathered together ready to leave, most of them with just a fraction of their possessions. The first of these were escorted past the fields of sunflowers to the village, and towards a line of buses and trucks destined to take them to the nearest railway station. Colonel Moscatelli arrived to say a formal goodbye to the Brigadier, but the seat reserved for him was empty, because he was one of the

---

6 Escape committee in POW camp

Within a POW camp, one officer was designated as the Escape Officer – he was charged with running the escape organization.

There was also an Intelligence Committee, which was responsible for the interrogation of new arrivals, and for the receipt and dispatch of coded messages. The Senior Allied Officer, on the advice of the Escape Officer and the Intelligence Officer, decided who would be allowed to escape. The Escape Committee was responsible for working out the details of how and when the attempt should be made.

prisoners who had chosen to hide away. Pandemonium ensued, and everything became lost in the confusion as a major search got underway.

Four hours later the convoy headed off, while a full scale search took place in the fortress. Colonel Moscatelli knew every nook and cranny of the fortress and he took an obvious delight in directing the Germans where to break down the internal walls, uncovering all the possible hiding places in the vast network of rooms and passageways. The four companions above the passage revealed themselves when they heard the Germans beneath them talking about tossing up a couple of grenades.

Eventually, all the prisoners were found, and they were locked into the lower compound for three days, where they consoled themselves with the contents of the Red Cross parcels they had hoarded so carefully. Now, special guards were brought in for their departure, from the battle hardened SS Feld-Gendarmerie. The prisoners were formed into a column, which headed out through the double grille and the entrance, en route to the German transit camp, in a stadium at Mantua and then to be entrained for Germany.

About 2,000 prisoners were assembled in the stadium, and during the course of their time in this large field, John and his friends were able to collect a few useful items from the troops, in particular a broken hacksaw blade and a dilapidated pair of pliers. They learned that a number of the men, who had managed to escape during the journey from Gavi, had reached Switzerland, only to be recaptured and handed back on the border. This meant that any escape from the train had to be made as early as possible, as plans to travel through Switzerland needed to be abandoned.

In due course, the officers were rounded up and herded into boxcars on a train that was headed for a camp deep inside Germany. These cattle trucks were standard in Europe at that time, the boxcars had slats between them, with flat beds alongside housing four mounted machine guns – one to shoot in each direction – and these were placed after every alternate car. The boxcars were wooden sided, and when the prisoners clambered on board the insides were wooden too.

There was only standing room for the forty two officers inside the truck, with no food, water or sanitary provision. The men, who had been incarcerated at Gavi, all had a history of escaping, and there was a real determination to overcome the obstacles they faced. In John's case, his knowledge of the dossiers about his activities was an extra spur. The men pooled the improvised implements they had secreted about their persons, such as escape saws, screwdrivers made from knives, and old bayonet tips.

Working in pairs, they beavered away until they had sawn through the wood at the end of the boxcar, to find that there was a steel plate behind the wood. It proved to be very difficult to remove the screws holding the plate, but working two at a time, they summoned up enough strength to remove them all during the course of the day. Now they had to saw quietly through the wooden cladding on the outside between their boxcar and the next one. The train had commenced the journey early in the morning, and by the time they were working on the outer wooden cladding, it was close to nightfall.

John was working on the wood when they finally broke through the wooden panel, leaving a hole of about 18 square inches. There was some consternation when the train came to a halt, and the guards started walking down the length of the trucks inspecting the train. Someone passed John a blanket, which he stuffed in the hole, and he and Bob Parrott held it in place.

Two by two, the men climbed out onto the buffers one facing each way. The plan was to jump, as soon as possible, on a given signal, when the train slowed for a bend. The first to jump should walk forward on the track, and the second man would walk back the way he had travelled until they met up, so that they could head for the border in pairs. John and Micky paired up; Micky, who was considerably smaller than John, wriggled through first, and then John followed. Micky thought that they should drop down between the two boxcars, but John thought this was too risky, and suggested that they should wait until the track was running beside a bank, enabling them to jump and roll down out of sight of the guards manning the machine guns. Standing on the buffers, with the telegraph poles whizzing past their eyes, they had to judge the delay between each of these to avoid falling onto the struts across the railway line. Micky jumped, and John counted the next pole and jumped on his side of the train. Unfortunately there was a signal attached to the pole and John collided with it. He fell clear but it was a severe bang. He fell into the ditch and when he regained consciousness he found that he was on his own. Then he 'hibernated', until he had recovered enough to start the long and arduous walk up into the mountains. Once again, he was relying on his navigation skills to head in the right direction, and once again, he was walking on his own in hostile territory. This time he only had a vague idea where he was starting from. The cut on his head did not give him much trouble after his initial recovery, but he had also damaged one of his hands, and he could see a protruding bone. This was a major problem, as his previous climb through mountains from France to Spain had necessitated hauling himself up some of the slopes by pulling on the vegetation. All the POWs in Gavi had a small haul of potentially useful items ready for their escape. John had managed to procure some sulphanilamide antibacterial crystals. He used these on his hand, and wrapped it in a handkerchief; he also managed to pull with his uninjured hand until the protruding bone clicked back into place.

John walked on his own up through the mountains, all the way to Friuli, where he was put in touch with Candido Grassi, who had taken the nom de guerre of Verdi. Grassi was among the first people in the area to organize a local anti-fascist group. Their initial aim was to encourage the Italian soldiers on the run to work with them, and avoid being deported to Germany as slave labour. Together with some priests from the local seminary, he wanted to organize a group that would fight and free themselves from fascism, but without ending up under communist rule. John was given messages for the Allies, asking for supplies and other assistance. He took the time, while he was there, to work out an appropriate drop zone, and a possible landing site for an aeroplane.

In due course, John was assisted on his way to link up with the communist partisans, through the border to Žiri in Yugoslavia, where he met two South Africans, who had also escaped. Žiri was an important town close to the border. A distinctive natural border runs along the hills west from the Žiri basin. In the period between the two world wars, there was a national border at Žiri between the kingdoms of Yugoslavia and Italy.

Aside from John, six other escapers jumped in the area south of Salzburg, near Golling. Micky Carmichael failed to find John, but met Jim Ratcliffe and they travelled together, jumping a goods train to Villach to make their way to the frontier near Tarvisio, then another to Udine, from where they walked to Medea and obtained civilian clothes.

On 7th October, they came across some partisans and met 'Major Temple' – Major Neville Lawrence Darewski, a British Liaison Officer[7] who represented Brigadier Fitzroy Maclean's military mission to Yugoslavia, tasked with attacking the communications hub of Carinthia. The following day, Ratcliffe volunteered to stay to help with the training of the Italian Partisans; on 16th October, he led the attack on a railway bridge,

---

7 British Liaison Officers

The British authorities kept in contact with the partisans through liaison officers sent by the intelligence services SIS and SOE. These small teams transmitted traffic by radio to their controlling stations in Cairo, Egypt and Bari, Italy.

just outside Santa Lucia, with a small band of partisans. They dressed in German uniforms, and took the guards by surprise. In the meantime, Carmichael, assisted by the partisans, went on as far as Žiri.

Bob Parrott, like John, didn't manage to rendezvous with his partner, so headed off on his own. Eventually he made contact with the anti-fascist movement, in the town of Schio, and was assisted as far as Žiri.

The men, who had escaped from the trains taking them from Gavi to Germany, decided to continue their travels together, with the help of the partisans. By now, bad weather had set in, and food was pretty scarce, so they became dependant on the partisans for their survival.

11

YUGOSLAVIA TO PENNA POINT

The partisans in Italy and Yugoslavia had complex backgrounds and aspirations, and now Micky Carmichael, Bob Parrott and John, with three other ranks (ORs), were together with the partisans in Žiri. They were in no position at the time to understand the complex situation of the people around them.

Slovenia was in the most northerly part of Yugoslavia. Before WW1 it formed part of the Hapsburg dominions and was administered partly by Hungary and partly by Austria. The Slovenians never forgot their heritage as a nation, and continued to speak their own language. In 1918, a provisional government was set up in Lubliana.

In Yugoslavia, the Serb monarchy ruled with Serbs in all the controlling positions in the army and the administration. This was resented by the Slovenes who were left with the junior clerical duties. When the Nazis conquered Yugoslavia, Slovenia came under oppressive Italian rule. Once the communist dominated partisan movement began, the Slovenes were quick to support it. When they joined the partisans, they became obstructive towards the escaping POWs who looked to them for help. The main purpose of the communists was to seize power in Yugoslavia after the war, so they built up an extensive organisation, which was far greater than was warranted by the operations they carried out.

Most of Slovenia was incorporated in Yugoslavia, but a large number of Slovenes came under Italian rule, as Italy was awarded land to the north east of the country, in acknowledgement of their loyalties during WW1. When Mussolini and his fascists rose to power in Italy, the Slovenians were dreadfully oppressed. The Slovenian economic, political and cultural organisations were demolished and banned. The use of the Slovenian language was prohibited; Slovenian place names were Italianised, and both Christian names and surnames were officially changed to Italian names. Under the fascists, the Slovenes faced a surge of unprecedented violence.

The Italian Communist Garibaldi band was active in the frontier area in Northeast Italy, namely Friuli Venezia Giulia, and cooperated with Tito's partisans on the Yugoslav frontier. The Garibaldi made no secret of the fact that they supported Tito's claim to absorb the Venezia Giulia Region into Yugoslavia after the war. The Garibaldi wore red handkerchiefs around their necks. The leaders of the Garibaldi partisans were communists, who had plenty of military experience, as they had taken part in the Spanish Civil War.

The whole group of prisoners and partisans were involved in a series of running fights by day and by night as they travelled for 60 kilometres. They ended up in a farmhouse in Sorica. The five officers and thirty seven other prisoners slept fitfully in a semi-derelict barn

Travelling on, marching in the daylight and sleeping in a variety of barns and outbuildings at night, they headed for Pobrdo (then called 'Piedecolle'). The problem was that they were surrounded by the German troops who had decided to clean up the area and were on the offensive, chasing them relentlessly through the snow. They were surviving on meagre rations and only ate once a day. Feeling cold, tired and hungry, they eventually set off on a nightmare march in a blizzard, at which point John and Micky lost the rest of the group. They dug into the snow on a precipice and stayed there for the night. Continuing the journey together, John and Micky bumped into a German sentry post. The sentry fired but missed. By now, the duo had learnt the art of bluff so they cursed the sentry in Italian for shooting at harmless peasants, whereupon the sentry retired inside the post. The following night they were able to shelter in a barn and were given some food before they collapsed into a deep sleep.

When they reached Italy, still close to the Yugoslav border, they were walking along a track when all of a sudden the bushes on both sides were pushed back, and they found themselves facing a couple of machine guns. They put their hands up and found that they had a major language barrier, though they tried English, French and Italian. They were taken away at gunpoint, and that night they were interrogated by the captain of the band, who bound their hands and feet and locked them in a wooden shack. Owing to the fact that many Slovenians in this area had resolutely resisted learning to use the Italian language, and had a deep hatred of the Germans without ever experiencing the German language, the captain decided that they must be German.

The following morning, they were given a shovel each and told to dig two trenches about six foot long and two foot wide. There was a machine gun trained on them all the time. The captain started haranguing his troops, and it was obvious that they were about to be executed. Two of the men gesticulated at them to remove their boots; presumably they didn't fancy removing them from two corpses. John and Micky decided that this was the end, and they quietly said their goodbyes to each other.

Suddenly, there was a kerfuffle down the road and the sound of cowbells, then a wagon appeared with the meagre daily meal; the soup was brought up from five miles away. The women delivering the meal called the men away from their grisly task to eat their dinner and John and Micky were thrown back into the shack where they had spent the previous night. Micky asked John how they were going to get out of this fix, and John told him that he would think of something. While their captors ate their meal there was the sound of a vehicle approaching. John was looking out through a gap in the wooden slats. He saw that the vehicle contained a British officer, and luckily John recognised him; it was Jim Radcliffe. John identified himself by shouting 'Ratty' through the gap, and Ratcliffe immediately convinced the captain of the partisans that the prisoners were his friends, and fellow escapees, and had them released into his care. The captain now insisted that the boots were returned to John and Micky, and that they were given something to eat. Even decades later, John shuddered as he remembered how horrible the soup had been.

A few days later, the two of them were able to join another band of partisans, and arrived at Caporretto (now Korabid). Here they joined other POWs who were with the Slovenian partisans, and they were interrogated before receiving false identity papers. Micky was given a photograph of his supposed fiancé Pepca, and he carried her photograph with his false identity card, which was in the name of Cimmino Filippo of Tarcenta. Now they hoped and expected, to receive assistance to make their way to reach the Allies.

The Slovenians were mainly Catholics, but between the two World Wars, the Italian authorities drove many of the priests out of their parishes, hoping that their replacements would be native born Italian priests, in an attempt to make the language of the Catholic Church entirely Italian. The Slovenian language had also been banned from all other important places. The Slovenians then began to turn against the Vatican for allowing this to happen, and individuals either adopted the Orthodox Church or became atheists, particularly the young. The communist party managed to collect large numbers of new members.

When Germany attacked and conquered Yugoslavia, the Slovenian part of Yugoslavia was divided, with Germany taking the large northern part, and Italy the smaller southern part with the capital Ljubliyana. After the Italian Armistice, all the Slovenian lands, which were annexed by Italy, according to the Treaty of Rapallo, came under the authority of the German military occupation, and formed part of the German military zone.

The partisans by now were an organised military force with two years' experience of guerrilla warfare. A British Liaison Officer had been in the area for more than a year, and since his arrival they had been recognised by the British Government, which was sending them supplies. However, there was no arrangement in place for evacuating escaped POWs who came into their territory. As far as the partisans were concerned, their need for recruits was of paramount importance, and they were willing to force the POWs to fight with them if they were unwilling to join them instead of rejoining their own forces. In these unfortunate circumstances, a number of the men joined the partisan bands as they needed shelter and food. They found themselves involved in hit and run fighting with insufficient arms, and inadequate clothing and food.

It was incomprehensible to the partisans that airmen had no military training, and were ill equipped to undertake long marches. To earn their keep, they were used to obtain food and supplies from the local population, who had little enough food for themselves and their families.

John, Micky, Bob and two South Africans were eventually passed to a Slovenian Battalion at Stupizza. Here they found a number of old friends, including Daniel Riddiford, who had been in the 'Cinque' with Bob and Major 'Stump' Gibbon who, together with Captain Peter Griffiths, had shared Bob's hidey-hole in the fortress in their attempt to escape from transportation to the Third Reich.

They were told that Griffiths had about thirty men under his command, holding part of the line near San Tietro in the foothills near Udine. It was not long before they all realized that they were virtual prisoners. There were about thirty other troops, with worn out boots. They were scantily clothed and had no greatcoats or blankets. The nights were very cold. When the officers remonstrated with the Battalion Commander, they received short shrift, and it became apparent that none of them were allowed to leave the village and it was impossible to get through the perimeter guard.

Griffiths reported that the underfed and underclothed men he commanded were being used to requisition supplies, so that the local Italian population blamed the British for their shortages. Differences in training and the language barrier resulted in confusion, making operations very difficult. The men had only taken up arms because they felt obliged to show their thanks for food and shelter, but now they just wanted to move on.

Major Gibbon and the South African Major Ballantine of 4th Field Company had paired up during their escape from the train. They took three weeks to walk together to Caporetto. They worked hard in negotiations with the partisan command at Caporetto for a safe conduct for the POWs through the partisan held Yugoslav territory to the Dalmatian coast. This was viewed as the defection of the British, so cooperation only came about after a very heated argument. In order to move on, the group needed a guide and armed escort to take them from one village to the next. For the time being they were all stuck in Stupizza.

One morning, the Germans bombed the next village, which was only about half a mile away. The order went out that if the aeroplanes appeared above, everyone should disperse up the side of the mountain; the village they were in was situated in a valley. Early the next morning, German bombers appeared in the sky, and Bob Parrott grabbed the opportunity to run past the guards and got clean away.

Once in the mountains, he encountered a partisan patrol who told him that their commander was an Englishman. These partisans were Serbs and more than willing to work with the British. They took him to their headquarters where he was delighted to find Jim Ratcliffe in charge. Ratcliffe informed him that the route home through Yugoslavia was open, and offered to provide food and place a guide at Parrott's disposal, if he felt able to walk the necessary distance to the British Military Mission HQ near Gorizia (a disputed border town, which at that time was under the administration of Yugoslavia's Istrian province). Parrott later wrote 'I thought this over and decided that here was a job I could do that would be both useful and exciting. Major Ratcliffe was an officer in whom I had the greatest amount of confidence and I had absolutely no hesitation in serving on his staff. I then informed him of the party of British Officers and Other Ranks, who were being detained by a hostile guerrilla leader. Ratcliffe immediately arranged for the Political Commissioner to send a message requesting the liberation of these men'.

Major Gibbon eventually headed up a group of five officers and about eighty ORs, they travelled east and slept in barns and lofts along the way, until they met a BLO whose instructions were to send all POWs to Major Jones (SOE's representative in Slovenia). The journey was not for the fainthearted, and impossible without adequate clothing and boots. The partisans arranged for the party to be divided into two, sending the first group on their way, and promising to equip the remaining men and send them on without delay.

When the first group reached Circhina, in Yugoslavia, Major Rupert Stuppel RAMC decided that, with the extreme shortage of medical aid among the partisans in the hills, he felt it his duty to stay on with them in his capacity as a doctor. He had, with two other doctors, tended admirably to the needs of his fellow POWs in Gavi, and they must all have been sorry to leave him behind. The rest of this group made a successful escape and arrived home in time for Christmas.

In the meantime, Ratcliffe brought Parrott up to date with his exploits since jumping from the train. Like John Mott he had slogged his way for twelve days, often without food, over extremely difficult terrain. This was through countryside full of enemy troops and with a hostile civilian population. Eventually he reached Udine, which was twenty five miles from the border; here he met a group of partisans who took him to the British Mission in Yugoslavia. Major Neville Darewski was a British Liaison Officer there, and Ratcliffe volunteered to return to Italy to form a battalion of partisans for service against the common enemy. His promotion to Major had been recommended, and he had arranged for the RAF to deliver supplies in the near future. Ratcliffe wore the badges of a captain but was known as 'the Commandant'. The strength of the battalion was about five hundred men. As well as training them, Ratcliffe had already led them in a number of successful actions against the enemy, including capturing about ten tons of flour. Confidence and morale was high, and they had just returned from an attack on a cement factory at Cannale.

The area was effectively the only route out of Italy into Yugoslavia, and the Germans maintained a mobile patrol on the roads, and a permanent guard on the bridge over the river Isonzo (now Soča). However, after a series of night attacks by the battalion, the Germans were compelled to withdraw into the cement factory each night. Consequently, movement in and out of Italy was greatly simplified, with free passage possible every night through Canalle, over the river Isonzo. Parrott trained about eighty men to act as a covering party for the demolition group, which Ratcliffe was instructing.

The news that British officers were commanding partisans brought many recruits into the camp. One day a complete Italian brigade arrived, including two hundred armed soldiers. The officers, including one full colonel, were not willing to serve under the partisans, but were eager and willing to serve under British officers.

A few days later, a quantity of demolition material was obtained, and they planned to blow up the railway bridge at Santa Lucia. Two nights later, having made their plans, they dressed in German uniforms and surrounded the bridge. With Major Ratcliffe in command, they took the bridge and its sixteen guards without any trouble. Parrott and his covering party were in two sections in some scrubland between the bridge and the road from Santa Lucia. After about two hours they received word of an approaching patrol. There were about thirty of them on the road. Parrott gave the order to fire and presumably inflicted heavy casualties, as they quickly withdrew and headed back the way they had come. Later, the Germans returned with machine guns and mortars, and subjected the party on the bridge to heavy fire. Parrott and his party attempted to close in on the bridge under cover of fire, but he received orders to withdraw to the RV (Rendezvous Point). On their way back, they heard an enormous explosion from the direction of the bridge. Both parties met up at the RV and went back up the mountainside with no more interference from the Germans. There was no way of knowing the casualty figures for the enemy, but their own casualties amounted to three killed and five wounded. The bridge was out of commission for quite a while.

Following this, morale rose to a peak, and large numbers of recruits continued to arrive; numbers increased to a brigade of two battalions, one of four hundred men, and one of two hundred. Now they had the manpower to blow up the road bridge at Stuppiza and one at Cividale, as well as two bridges on the Udine to Gorizia line. This activity protected the flank of the brigade from any German heavy artillery; they then closed in on the railway line, which ran from Udine to Tarvisio, where the German defensive line was based. For several nights, a machine gun party went into the embankment and gunned the trains from close range. The value of this action was high, and at one point no trains went through for four nights. When the night service resumed, all trains were prefaced by an armoured car and a pilot engine. This kind of warfare suited the partisans down to the ground and their spirited action against the Germans augured well for the future. All that was needed to turn the brigade into a first class fighting force was for the RAF sortie bringing stores to arrive. During this time, Ratcliffe and Parrott were able to pass a number of British ORs safely into the hands of the British Mission.

Ratcliffe was now contacted by a very large underground movement calling itself the 'Liberali'. It consisted of many officers, students and professional men, some of whom held positions of trust under the Germans and fascists. They could operate in all the large towns in Northern Italy, so Ratcliffe persuaded them to stay underground, and to use their organisation to collect and pass on all possible information, which could then be relayed to the British Mission for transmission to British GHQ.

Ratcliffe had made an urgent appeal to the British Mission outlining the situation in Northern Italy, and had asked for demolition stores for use against aircraft and railway engines. The brigade had access to the goods yard at Udine, and to an aerodrome nearby, where more than twenty five six engine aeroplanes were being serviced. All this knowledge came from the Liberali. One of these requests had been given to Major Gibbon to give to the British Mission, as he left after the detention of his group in Stuppiza.

Bob Parrott wrote:

'Everything depended on this sortie arriving. We badly needed our own transmitter and we wanted explosives, arms and ammunition. We were always being told of the Russian advances and we wanted something tangible to show that the Government was behind us. A six day window was given for the RAF sortie to arrive; the signal fires were lit and the long wait commenced. We waited for seven nights to no avail and eventually we had to admit that the stores were not going to arrive. Ratcliffe and I went to a meeting with the leaders of the Liberali. They, by the way, were our only contact as there was no blood lost between the Liberali and the communist partisans. Ratcliffe had sent the other members of the Liberali away as they were perturbed to discover that arms supplied to the communists had been stored away for use against the established government in Italy after the Germans had gone and it was best that at this time there should be no open friction. Ratcliffe told the Liberali that, as the stores had not arrived, he would go over the mountains to the British Mission himself to find out about the sortie and to hand in all the information they had given us so that it could be sent to the British GH and to try and bring back a transmitter. I was to be in charge for ten days after which, if Ratcliffe had not returned, I was to order the Brigade to break up into small parties and to keep undercover until fresh orders arrived. I was then to follow on to the British Mission, having first picked up the latest despatches and information from the Liberali. This had to be done secretly as we did not want the partisans to know of our meeting owing to the nature of the information'[8]

The weather deteriorated over the next week or so, snow kept falling and lying thickly on the ground. Bob carried out his instructions and left for Yugoslavia. He crossed the Isonzo River to Circhina where he learnt from the civil population of the death of a British Major, and of another one being wounded in a Stuka raid, which had been carried out on the town. It appeared to have been a deliberate attack on the partisan hospital. He later wrote:

'Everybody I met was full of praise and admiration for the Major Doctor who, it appeared, had done some magnificent work in the area. Without any regard for his personal safety, he had administered to the sick and wounded in the hospital, and had made dangerous journeys to the needy in the field when his services had been required. He was credited with saving many lives and it did my heart good to hear of an Englishman who had held such a warm place in the hearts and memories of these people. I can honestly say that his conduct had done a lot to maintain the morale of the people.

I later learned that the deceased officer was Major Rupert Stuppel RAMC. During the bombing of the town, his hospital was hit and the doctor and another officer were seen to leave cover and run towards the hospital, apparently to extricate the wounded partisans. They stopped a bomb between them, Major Stuppel was killed and the other officer, Major Ratcliffe, was wounded. Although I reached headquarters, I was unable to find the British Major in charge of the Mission. I was told that he had left the area, on the day of the bombing, leaving all his gear

---

8 Information en route to the BM included the knowledge that two German divisions were coming into the mountains to clean up the partisans; Field Marshall Rommel was going to Belgrade and a large scale map of Udine with a number of important points marked.

behind and had not returned. I stayed in the area for two or three days and then decided to make my way home. I crossed into Yugoslavia and met Captains Allan Yeoman, E. Wilson and Flight Lieutenants John Mott and Micky Carmichael, with about thirty troops. The Germans had, it seemed, decided to clean up the area and were on the offensive. We were unable to go forward and, as it turned out, unable to return, for the whole area was ringed by Germans. For the next ten days, we were with a Brigade of partisans and were chased mercilessly day and night, up and down mountains in thick snow and averaging one poor meal a day.

It was a very poor end to my schemes. We officers had a conflab and decided that the best thing we could do was to get back to Italy, so we presented this idea to the Brigade Commander, who received it very coldly but after an argument, lasting about three days, we won our point and obtained the passes we desired.'

The next time the Germans attacked, Bob broke off quickly from the partisans; doing a sharp movement round and behind them, he headed for the Tarvisio tunnel and Italy.

'Things were going quite well for me when, unfortunately, a German stepped out from behind a tree and I found that I had walked into a patrol and was once more in the bag. I was handed over to the SS in a small village where we found Captains Allan Yeoman and E Wilson and about fifteen troops. We were continually being called partisans and bandits by the SS troops and told that we would be shot and I must say that, tired and run down as we were after a very gruelling fortnight, we began to believe them. That night, however, I was interrogated by a young SS Oberleutnant and, after two hours or more, I managed to convince him that we were not partisans or bandits, we had not carried arms, we had not interfered with the Germans in any way and that we were only poor POWs trying to reach our own lines after the armistice in Italy. We were put into trucks and taken to a transit camp after a rest of four days we journeyed into Germany in time to arrive for Christmas.'

The partisan Brigade Commander came up with an idea involving the remaining POWs. He planned to attack Trieste and get rid of the Germans. He told them that the British POWs would be the spearhead of the attack as they were trained soldiers, so they asked him for some ammunition – they were offered ten rifles and six rounds of ammunition for each of these; this was to attack a general garrison, and was to take place the following day. Faced with this impossible situation, the officers went back to their shelters in the snow and discussed with the troops what they should do. The decision was made that the only way out of this was to leave in twos or threes at two minute intervals during the cover of darkness. Micky and John decided to change tack and attempt to reach the Allied lines in Italy; they went off about the third or fourth pair, heading northwards, until they got into the mountains.

Their endurance was severely tested when they were faced with a river that they needed to cross. There was no sign of a boat, but there was a 'bucket cable' overhead. The bucket was on the opposite bank but they failed to shift it despite their best efforts, so they had to make their way across monkey fashion. Micky reached the bank, but John fell in completely exhausted. Fortunately, he was not far from the bank, so the water, though icy, was only about four feet deep; Micky hauled him out. It was just as well that John's great friend was on hand to rescue him. A far cry from when he had fallen into the water as a schoolboy, this time there was no big brother to lead him to a hot bath followed by tea and cake.

The duo had bypassed Trieste and now climbed out of the valley and up onto a precipice. There was a sheer drop when they reached the top and they could see no way forward except to launch themselves off, and hope for a soft landing. John found it very difficult to follow this through, but Micky called out to him to follow and jumped into thin air. This gave John the courage to follow suit and they both landed safely far below their launch point.

Eventually, they reached a lone house about ten miles from the university town of Udine. An elderly gentleman answered their knock on the door and made them welcome. He spoke good English, which he told them he had learned when he attended the university. His house was full of books in a variety of languages. He and his wife lived in splendid isolation in his family home. The only time he had ever been away from home had been when he attended the university. Now, he only ventured out to buy books. Once he had learned English, he had no trouble learning other languages in order to read the books he obtained.

For a while, John and Micky travelled with an American evader and a couple of soldier escapers. One of these was a very fat Scot, known as Jock, but he couldn't tolerate anything Italian, so they parted company with this particular trio. Fortunately, they were taken in hand by a farmer, who sheltered them, in spite of the proximity of the Germans.

In mid December, the duo reached Treppo Grande, where they spent a week with the Tea family. The husband and wife lived with two daughters and a niece, and they had one main living room that served all the needs of the family. When John and Micky arrived in their dishevelled, and somewhat dirty state, a bath was hauled in front of the fire and filled with hot water. This was hugely welcome, but it was a bit disconcerting to bathe in front of the whole family. However, the welcome was wonderful and the family generously shared their food and beds.

The Italians who assisted the escapers took huge personal risks. Those in the countryside were known as the Contadini, and they fed, hid and guided the men in spite of the scarcity of food and the dreadful punishments inflicted by the Germans. Their staple diet was polenta, which was traditionally made with cornflour, but in dire times it was made with chestnut flour, or ground walnuts. Water was added, and then the mixture was boiled until it formed a thick paste, which was spread on the table. A topping was added using any foodstuffs that were available (not much in the depths of winter), then the family all ate together. Coffee was made with ground acorns or roasted barley.

Food was limited and with little variety during the course of their whole escape journey. For much of the time, their diet was a constant of cooked dried beans or chestnuts, with the only fresh salad consisting of green dandelion leaves. Chestnuts were an important part of people's diets at that time, eaten either in soups, ground into flour, or roasted over the fire. Years after the war, when it became fashionable to serve Christmas turkeys with 'luxury chestnut stuffing', John could never bring himself to even think about it, let alone eat it.

Christmas came and went. John had no idea that the first partisans he had encountered were now formed into a group called The Osoppo. The Osoppo partisans were founded on Christmas night 1943, by Don Ascanio De Luca, who was the former Chaplain of the Alpini in Montenegro, and was now at the local seminary, where he became the political leader. The Commander was Candido Grassi (Verdi) and Manlio Cencig (Mario) was his deputy; they were both captains of the Italian Army.

They located the headquarters of the brigade in the Pielungo castle, in Val d'Arzino. The Osoppo was mainly composed of Alpine troops who had been serving in the frontier areas before the armistice. They wore green scarves around their necks. Obviously they were anti-Fascist and anti-Nazi, but most importantly they were anti-Communist.

The Osoppo Partisan Brigade operated under the orders of the Committee of Liberation, which was formed to coordinate the resistance to German occupation by disparate partisan groups of diverse political persuasions. The Committee of Liberation consisted of the political parties that had been in hiding since their suppression by Mussolini in 1922. Their first acts were to aid escaping Allied POWs and deserters from the Italian army.

At times the Garibaldi and the Osoppo did work together in a limited way towards their common goal of defeating the Nazis and Fascists. However, this was all to come to an end when the Garibaldini became an integral part of Tito's IX Slovene Corps.

Meanwhile, John and Micky, who were now in a group of five, walked twenty five miles to Valvazone from where they took an overnight train to Bologna, accompanied by an Italian Officer. They took two further overnight train journeys together and then there was a long walk before they reached Forlimpopoli. They continued to trudge for twelve days in the snow, and with a constant cold wind, until they found shelter in a cowshed and slept in the most welcome and comfortable hay. On the 6th January, they were given a bed in a farm near to a Monastery, and the following day they were met by Dr. Carlo Bertello, who originally came from Sicily. He arranged to have their dilapidated shoes repaired, which made a huge difference to them. Over the next few days they were able to get their clothes washed and on 12th January, they saw the first Spitfires in the sky. A few days later they came across Major Lugio, who promised to help with securing a boat for them to sail down the Adriatic. This came to nothing, and they had reason to believe that he reverted to his original fascist sympathies. For the last few days of the month, the group stayed with Rita Guiseppe at Campo Largo in Petriolo, but when Major Lugio did not reappear, they abandoned the plans to purchase the promised boat, and the group shared out the money they had gathered, before splitting up and going their separate ways. John and Micky wrote carefully worded letters to their parents and entrusted them to Rita, who undertook to post them to England. The letters reached their destinations in November 1944.

The families, who sheltered the duo, usually tried to find a shed or barn where they could sleep, so that any raid on the part of the Germans would not identify their helpers. The most welcome bedding was hay, as it was so warm, and this was often aided by animals sheltering underneath the hay loft. Sometimes they were given scuss mattresses. These were made of maize husks and resulted in a reasonable sleep. Piles of mulberry or chestnut leaves did not stay secure, and usually resulted in waking up very cold. Sleeping on straw was scratchy and not very warm, but they were always grateful to be sheltered from the elements. In one house where they were offered shelter, Micky became concerned when he realised that there were no provisions for coping with bodily functions. Once the family understood his needs, he was directed to a communal privy at the end of the village. To his consternation, a local woman entered after him, and sat beside him, as though it was the most natural thing in the world.

At the beginning of February, initial contact was made with Countess Ganucci at Belmonte Piceno, and she agreed to lend them sufficient money to purchase a boat, for which they would sign a promissory note to be redeemed after the end of the war. These notes came to be known as 'Churchill's chitties', and they were indeed honoured after the cessation of hostilities.

A determined group of escapers came together at this stage, and they divided up the tasks necessary to complete their plans to sail down the Adriatic, until they reached the Allied lines. By now, the two friends had joined up with Lt Ian Bain of the 1st Worcestershire, who had some experience as a sailor, Capt RC Matthews SACS, Cpl JGW Lipscombe CMP, and Sgt WV Ott US Airborne.

Reliant on friendly Contadini farming families for shelter and food, they heard rumours that a farmer had a hidden boat that had been found by fisherman off shore. It turned out to be a small German whaler, and was pointed at one end like the lifeboat of a ship. John was detailed to borrow a bicycle and return to the Countess to collect the promised 25,000 Lira. They took the money to the farmer, who showed them the boat, which was hidden under a haystack, but it had no oars or sails; these he could obtain at a cost of 5,000 Lire.

The group split into two. Ian Bain led one group, preparing the boat as best they could, while the others went out and about to make the additional money that was needed. The number of men in the group had now grown to nine, one or two of them had already learnt the art of trading on the black market and they knew that if they stole goods which had been requisitioned from the Italians off the German transport wagons, they could easily sell these same goods back to them. By this means the group managed to obtain the extra money.

Micky was carrying a large Italian touring map on the back of which he was keeping a cryptic log; years after the war, Micky's father sought John's help in interpreting and expanding the details on this precious document.

By now the group had grown to include Sgt FA Rawlings RAF, Cpl HJ Sergeant RE (Jimmy), and Cpl WG Cook RE (Wally).

The farmer's wife dyed the sails blue, so that they would be less obvious when at sea, and the farmer also obtained mast, boom, gaff, tiller and cordage, everything at a price. When they asked about a compass, the farmer told them that he had a suitable maritime compass, but it would cost them. By now they were thoroughly fed up with his greed, so they found out where it was hidden and took it. Between them, they gathered together sufficient stores to keep them going for three days. These were stowed on board with the rest of the equipment.

Ian Bain had a fair amount of sailing experience so he was designated skipper, and John and Micky were designated navigators. They did not give any hint of their lack of previous sailing experience. They had each had toy sailing boats as children, and John had once spent a day sailing in Poole Harbour. However, they were both highly skilled navigators.

The scheme was now complete, and all was set for a departure on the night of 17th March. Their host, Giovani, saw them on their way in twos and threes, while it was still night heading for Strada Nat. At dusk they could see the farmhouse where the boat was hidden on the opposite side of the road. One at a time, they crossed the road at the ferry signal station. The necessary final preparations took under an hour. While these were in progress, John had to work hard to persuade the farmer to use his oxen to tow the boat across the fields to the water. At one point, they had to cross the main railway line, and just as they were about to make the crossing, a troop train approached. Hastily, they herded the cattle around the boat, and crouched down between the beasts so that the animals would appear to be grazing. All went well until grass became sand, and the oxen could not keep their footing. At this point, the farmer unhitched them and headed back. Now deserted and in the dark, the men had to pull out some boundary posts and create a wooden pathway to the water's edge, then roll the boat over this contraption. Pushing and pulling, they finally made it, and clambered on board in high spirits, in spite of the very cramped conditions. Jimmy and Wally set to work with muffled oars, and made slow progress out to sea. About half an hour later, they heard a train pass, and then a watercraft passed between them and the shore. The water was completely calm, and for this brief interlude, everyone was in high spirits and set about rigging the sails.

The compass proved to be all but useless, as it did not contain any liquid. These compasses are traditionally filled with isopropyl alcohol. Isopropyl alcohol is very volatile; it will find any weakness in the seals and evaporate. One member of the group told the others that he had heard somewhere that urine would make a suitable substitute. This was provided, and the compass then functioned as intended. They set sail eastwards and were delighted to be truly underway.

By morning, the wind had freshened, and they started to move more swiftly towards their destination. A German aeroplane, passing overhead, caused some slight concern, but their attention was drawn to the state of the sails. As soon as the wind got up it became apparent that they were not sails at all. The farmer's wife had dyed ordinary bed sheets, and sewn them into the shape of sails, with no regard for the fact that these men would be reliant on the finished product. Any guilty consciences the men might have felt about removing the fence posts from the field vanished, and were replaced by anger at the way in which they had been duped. The sails were only the start of their problems; four of them became horrifically seasick and the remainder felt far from well. Experiences since their various escapes meant that they were not a group of fit individuals to start with, and now all nine of them were feeling the strain of being out at sea, confined in this very small boat, which was exposed to the elements and to the enemy.

When night fell there were sounds of other craft in the near vicinity, then they heard someone hail them, and immediately ceased all activity, drifting until they thought that they had gained some distance from the source. The wind freshened again and they made record progress. They saw flashes of 'Arty' and began to assume that they must be near the line. Now the seasickness took hold again and tempers began to fray. When the wind dropped, they took to the oars, but none of them were now fit enough to make much impact. In the morning, a few fishing boats were sighted, and some in the group became convinced that they had travelled far enough down the coast to have reached the line. There was a heated debate with the two navigators, who were hoping to get a fix on a landmark to verify their position; faced with a near mutiny they set course for the shore. Over the next few hours, progress was very slow, as the men were all in pretty poor shape by now, and the seasickness had taken its toll. They approached the shore with caution, and made landfall at 3.30pm only to be confronted by a detachment of Gurkhas from the 5th Indian Division. These fighting men were armed with the most recognizable and famous fighting knives ever developed. John, faced with a man brandishing a kukri, was terrified, and later wrote that it was the most frightening moment of his life. The leader of the patrol took them prisoner, and placed them under armed guard in a tent, where they lay down on camp beds completely exhausted.

A British Army officer was watching their arrival from outside his tent, where he was having a shave after taking a nap. He was behind the front line recovering from a flesh wound received at the current Battle of Monte Cassino. Gazing out to sea, while he shaved desert style, mug of water in one hand and razor in the other, he reflected on the relentless series of battles he had been involved in since joining up in India, where he had been living when the war broke out. His thoughts turned to his family as he watched the Gurkhas bring in the bedraggled group of prisoners. He pondered on the fact that one of them walked in a way that reminded him of his brother, now a prisoner of war somewhere in France. Just as he was leaving his tent, the Gurkha patrol leader approached him to say that one of the prisoners had given the same name as him. Pip Mott grabbed his hat and hurried to the tent where John was being held. Lifting the flap, he poked his head in and asked John what he was doing there. John replied, in trained and formal fashion, explaining that they were all POWs who had escaped. Pip interrupted to say that he would immediately ask his Brigadier for a couple of days' leave, and then the penny dropped. The last time these two brothers had seen each other was five years previously, when Pip had set sail for India to seek his fortune in February 1938.

The atmosphere in the tent changed immediately and the men were soon rejuvenated by the thrill of English company, cigarettes and tea. Afterwards they had photos taken of the crew and craft.

THE PITCH AND TOSS
COURTESY OF THE MERCIAN REGIMENT MUSEUM (WORCESTERSHIRE) – ORIGINALS
FROM THE MOTT FAMILY COLLECTION

12

FROM PENNA POINT TO REPATRIATION

The weary travellers had a good night's sleep then Pip Mott was detailed to debrief his brother, but John's first priority was to deliver the crucial messages he had received from the partisans in the Friuli region, who he had met on his solo journey towards Yugoslavia the previous September.

This was timely indeed, although its importance was not immediately apparent. John and Micky had made good use of their time in Macerata. They had carefully explored the area so that they could pinpoint possible bombing targets and, in addition, they were able to report on the enemy's Castelfidaro barracks at Macerata, along with the smaller barracks in the western area. This information was put to good use, and the barracks were subsequently destroyed in a bombing raid by the RAF.

When they eventually returned to England, both John and Micky were awarded the MBE.

Pip Mott's daughter Judy remembers her father telling her when she was a child that her Uncle John had arrived with 'some very useful information'. This understatement was typical of all three of the Mott brothers, but it was also the case that knowledge of 'secret' information was strictly limited to the relevant departments. When the restrictions were lifted, decades later, most ex-servicemen had become so used to observing the secrecy rules that it simply didn't occur to them to reveal the knowledge they had kept to themselves for so long. As Pip once said, they had been 'trained to forget'.

When Pip's Brigadier was made aware of the brother's reunion, he gave him a 48 hour pass and provided a truck and Gurkha driver. Pip and John caught up with all their news during the journey to Naples, arriving at around dusk on the 21st March 1944. As they completed their journey they were greeted by the impressive sight of Mount Vesuvius in action; smoke and ash were rising to a height of 20,000 feet. Dust and ashes were falling like rain on the neighbouring village of Torre di Grecco. The two of them had a brilliant time that weekend, then Pip went back to fight his war, and John was delivered to the ex-POW collection unit at Naples where he rejoined Micky and the others. Soon after their arrival, John received orders to report to Cairo, and an American aircraft was sent to Naples to collect John and Micky to fly them to Bigna. At this point Micky was repatriated. When he reached Cairo, John found himself in the company of the other two RAF Flight Lieutenants with the surname Mott. One of them had been brought from The Far East and one from West Africa. Once the authorities had established that it was John they wished to speak to, the other two were returned to base. John was questioned about all aspects of his time with the partisans; he was then transferred to No.1 Special Force at Bari, in Italy, to assist the British agents who were now attached to the SOE Operation BALLOONET, which was a political and military mission to the East Tyrol. The agents were busy preparing for Operation AUNSBY.

Churchill had always believed that there was a good case to be made for using the Ljubljana Gap to advance into Central Europe. Once the Americans came into the war, their influence eventually led to the centring of all the resources on the D-Day Operation, but Churchill still felt that conquering Vienna using his original plans was a valid course of action. Together with the British Army chiefs, he kept developing plans that needed the support of the local partisans. However, the Garibaldi partisans were growing ever closer to Tito's partisans who, in turn, were building stronger relationships with the Soviets.

There were no active SOE Operations in Austria before 1943. Then a Mission, code-named 'CLOWDER', was charged with infiltrating men into Austria, and assisting the resistance groups that they hoped to find. The SOE agents posted to this mission were working with the help of the communist partisans. It wasn't long before it became apparent that the main aim of these partisans was the annexation of the territory claimed by Yugoslavia, whereas the Allies had only one objective, and that was to defeat the Germans.

CLOWDER was run from SOE London, and was completely independent from Fitzroy Maclean's SOE mission in Yugoslavia. The story of Major Gibbon's exploits had led to the belief that this mission could be established successfully in the area. In spite of the best efforts of all involved, the goals of sabotage and subversion in Austria, within the Third Reich, were never achieved, but valuable information was obtained, and gave an independent assessment of the activities and capabilities of the communist partisans.

In 1938, the Austrian population had welcomed the Werhmacht, and the country became an extension of the Third Reich. All men of a suitable age were absorbed into the military, and it took quite a while for the Austrians to realize that it was the Germans who ended up with the senior ranks, and the important positions in public life were reserved for Germans who were brought into Austria. Although the population felt aggrieved by this situation and the anti-Catholic measures that were taken, there was no inclination to take any significant action against them. Fear of Nazi reprisals meant that the sum total of resistance that the majority of these dispirited people were prepared to take was the passive action of dressing in the Austrian national colours, alongside maintaining the traditional Austrian greeting of 'Grüß Gott' rather than using 'Heil Hitler'.

Churchill wanted to find a way to infiltrate men into Austria to make contact with any Resistance groups that might exist, without involving the communists. He was looking for a back door into Central Europe, to see if there might still be a way of ensuring that British or American troops would arrive in Vienna ahead of the Russians. All three powers were still Allies, with the joint aim of fighting to overcome Germany, but it had now become necessary to consider the position of the countries in Central Europe when the war came to an end.

Number 1 Special Force had come into being in September 1943, after the armistice. SOE activities were placed under the command of Gerry Holdsworth, who chose the codename Maryland as a tribute to his wife. The headquarters was based in Southern Italy at Monopoli, near Bari, on the Adriatic coast. 1 SF had exclusive responsibility for all SOE operations mounted from Italy into enemy occupied territory, and they were directly responsible to the government through their own headquarters in London, under the Ministry of Economic Warfare. It was neither part of IS9, nor of the intelligence service.

Austria was included in its responsibilities rather than falling within the Mediterranean command.[9]

The character of SOE's task had changed fundamentally. The principle tactical requirement of 1 SF was to cause the maximum interference with the enemy's lines of communication, directing the activities of the partisans with the plans of the military HQ. Another important aspect of their work was supplying the partisans by air. It assisted with the evacuation of escaped POWs and evading airmen, and sometimes assisted in the gathering of intelligence, though it was quite independent of the bodies responsible for those functions. It also helped by disseminating rumours and black propaganda, with the aim of undermining the morale of the enemy.

When John's debriefing report reached the powers that be, it provided information that would lead to an opportunity for SOE to work with non-communist partisans in the Friuli area. The significance of the area had been recognised, but the problem was with the access. Now, there was this report from an RAF escaper with details of such partisans who wished to help the Allies, and details about suitable drop zones, plus a possible landing area. John had noted that there was a short area of flat land between the sea and the mountains. His credentials as a Special Duties Lysander pilot, with all its implied skills, meant that John's journey home was put on hold.

John's solo sojourn with a group of these partisans had taken place before they had become part of the Osoppo, who were formed at the Church of Pozzis on Christmas night 1943, on the advice of don Graziano, the parish priest of Verzegnis. The non-political Osoppo was mainly made up of lay Catholics and included men from Alpini regiments serving in the frontier areas before the armistice. Candido Grassi was a Professor of Art who had been a captain in the army; he was their Commander and his nom de guerre was 'Verdi'.

Friuli was hugely important. Situated in Italy's most north eastern region, it borders Austria to the north and Slovenia to the east. To the south it faces the Adriatic Sea, and to the west its internal border is with the Veneto region. Immediately after the armistice, in September 1943, Hitler proclaimed two separate zones directly under German command: The Tirol and the Adriatic Littoral, which included Friuli. These zones were vital to the control of the lines of communication for supply to the German

---

9 IS9 mainly represented the interests of MI9, the branch of the War Office responsible for organising the escape and evasion of Allied personnel from enemy occupied territory.

forces in Italy. Friuli lay close to the area claimed by Yugoslavia. From the perspective of the allies, it was the gateway to Austria. The river Tagliamento ran through a valley, which divided the area into two, with the Osoppo partisans operating to the west of the river.

The Osoppo Partisan Brigade operated under the orders of the Committee of Liberation, which was formed to coordinate the resistance to German occupation by disparate partisan groups of diverse political persuasions. The Committee of Liberation consisted of the political parties that had been in hiding since their suppression by Mussolini in 1922. Their first acts were to aid escaping Allied POWs and deserters from the Italian army. Tensions between the Catholics and the communists in the movement led to the foundation of the Fiamme Verdi.

By the middle of 1944, the resistance had cleared almost all the German garrisons out of the mountains between the plain and the Austrian border. This meant that they were always at risk of attack as the Germans tried to regain control. There was an anticipation of an Allied breakthrough, after the fall of the Fascist regime, and the same expectations began to stir some Austrians to believe that the Nazi occupation might be coming towards its end.

The SOE Operation BALLOONET was tasked with making a reconnaissance of the frontier of the Austrian Tirol, to explore the possibilities of infiltrating agents into Austria from Northern Italy. It was also a clandestine mission, under firm instructions to avoid all contact with the enemy, and to disguise its true purpose by claiming its task was to help exfiltrate ex-Allied prisoners of war to safety. The mission members were strictly forbidden by their superiors from meddling with political questions, especially with the most sensitive one concerning the demarcation between Yugoslavia and Italy. However, they were asked to report regularly on the political situation in the field.

At the time when the plans were being formulated, Squadron Leader Count Manfred Czernin had completed his training with 1 SF, and was awaiting orders. He had a distinguished career as a pilot, serving through the Battle of Britain, but had been invalided home after over 1000 flying hours. His father was from one of the leading families within the Austro-Hungarian Empire. Born in Germany, his parents separated when he was just one year old, and his mother took him to live in Italy. At the age of seven he was sent to boarding school in England. Manfred used his mother's maiden name of Becket as his code name, and he spoke both Italian and German with ease. Once he had received his initial briefing, he waited for his partner to arrive.

Captain Patrick Martin-Smith arrived at the Mess in Monopoly on a motorbike to meet Manfred. He was a Cambridge graduate, who had been with the commandos, and was then brought to Solerno with an intelligence unit. He was now due to be transferred to the Austrian section of 1SF as a German speaker, who also spoke Italian.

John was transferred to 1 SF and was brought from Cairo to Bari so that the two agents could 'pick his brains' as Pat Martin-Smith later wrote. John described the nature of the partisans and the area where he had been. His information centred on the village of Clauzetto, northwest of Udine. Having gleaned all the information available, the decision was made to travel in two parties, first Czernin and his radio operator Lieutenant De Felice 'Piero', then, one month later, Martin-Smith and his operator Charles. In this way, Manfred would be able to see the lie of the land, and call for any extra items to be brought by the second party.

Operation AUNSBY was the start of the process of establishing the required dispatch posts on the Austrian border. John was involved with the commencement of Operation AUNSBY and on 9th June, he was a crew member on Halifax JP248 of 624 Squadron with F/Sgt McColl in command. Their route took them from Brindisi – Yugoslavia – Austria – Friuli – Base, but the trip was only partially successful, owing to the weather. On 11th June, John was on the crew with F/O Mareweski, flying the Halifax JP317on the same route, and this time the drop for Operation AUNSBY was successful. Who or what was dropped from this particular aeroplane is not recorded in any available record.

Czernin and Martin-Smith had a hair-raising time carrying out their mission. Czernin was eventually brought out by Lysander from the landing strip, which he had been able to confirm was suitable. During the months that he spent operating in the region, he was able to make use of Piero's skills with the radio, so could send reports back to base whenever he needed to do so. However, in a complete break from accepted practice, he made use of a courier to take a highly secret written report to Florence en route to No 1SF at Monopoly.

Renato del Din was a founder member of the Osoppo partisans, who died when leading a surprise attack in Tolmezzo. His sister, Paola, then offered her services to continue the work that he had believed in so passionately. The twenty-one-year-old took his name as her adopted code name. She was a fourth year student at Padua University, having transferred her studies from Bologna University, when travelling became too difficult. She had carried out a number of missions for Fiamme Verdi before Verdi sent for her on 22nd July, he instructed her to carry secret documents to the Allies, three hundred miles south to Florence. Her mother gave her consent to the mission, and made a special pouch for the documents so that they could be hidden under Paola's clothes. When she met Czernin, he told her that the contents of the package could help to shorten the war, and he then sent a signal through Piero, giving her details and the date she was due to leave Udine.

Paola headed off on her dangerous journey, staying first at the convent in Padua where she had stayed while at the university. Her journey progressed from this convent to another, where her sister had stayed while studying. Seeking help on her journey, she even managed to look young and vulnerable enough to be assisted by some Germans whom she encountered on the way. On arrival in Florence, she tried to contact a professor whose son had been a close friend of Renato's. Florence was at the centre of a battle being fought street by street, with dreadful damage being inflicted on many homes and other buildings. The professor and his wife had no facilities to offer her, but he accompanied her to the Sacred Heart College where she sheltered until the Germans took over the building.

Paola moved on to stay with some monks, and it was here that she heard that one of them had a Red Cross pass to escort a patient to hospital in the part of the city controlled by the Allies. Eventually, she persuaded the Germans to allow her to accompany the patient as well. Once the trio were met by two British officers, she was taken to the British High Command at the Hotel Excelsior. Here, she produced her passport and Czerin's letter of introduction. The papers she delivered from Czernin included a long report in Italian from Verdi. When she was debriefed, she passed on some of her own useful observations. Paola was flown to Monopoly, where she expressed a determination to return home and continue her work. To facilitate this, she was sent on a parachute course, and was eventually dropped back into the Udine area, where she continued her work as a skilled courier. In recognition of her gallant actions she was awarded the Medaglia d'Oro al Valor Militare, the same award that had been given to her brother posthumously.

During his stint with 1 SF, John completed four operations, bringing his wartime total to 23. It was with mixed emotions that he assisted with a supply drop to the very partisan group who had so nearly executed Micky and him, some months earlier. His only recorded comment about this time reads; 'I was called to Cairo for attachment to No.1 Special Force at Bari, in Italy, to assist in the delivery of supplies by air to the partisans in Yugoslavia. After two months with No. 1 Special Force at Bari, I was repatriated to England.'

While John was away from home, the other members of the family were coping with one difficulty after another. His parents were very stressed, as there had been no contact with John or Pip for a while. The house in Marchmont Road suffered bomb damage and was uninhabitable. Consequently, Arthur and Florence stayed temporarily at a different address, a little further out of the main town, and mail went astray. John ended up addressing his mail to the local Westminster Bank. The day after Pip and John met in Italy, Mervyn was posted to HMS Turtle in Poole. Here, secret preparations were underway for the D-Day landings. Shortly after this, Frances and her cousin, together with the two young children plus a babe in arms, emerged from the Morrison shelter at their house in Wallington, to find the ceiling was on top of the shelter, and the house had suffered severe damage from a doodlebug. Hitler had been fooled by some black propaganda that led him to believe that his rockets were overshooting London. The end result of this was that the suburbs in Surrey and Kent were bombarded by these destructive bombs instead of London. The family were evacuated to Hamworthy, near Poole, and shortly after this, Arthur took early retirement before he and Florence moved to the family bungalow in East Meon, in Hampshire.

In the meantime, Pip was embroiled in the Fourth Battle of Monte Cassino; the key position of Santa Angelo fell on 13th May, to a combined Ghurkha and 11th Canadian Tank B Squadron attack. Then the British and Indian divisions went over the Rapido River, south of Cassino, and took up a position on the opposite side. The 8th Indian Division conquered the town of Pignataro. At sunrise, on 18th May, the monastery hill was in Allied hands, and the battles of Monte Cassino were finally over. On 1st June, Mervyn led the parade of the personnel heading off from HMS Turtle to the D-Day landings.

John's journey home from Italy took five days. On 21st June he was flown in a Mitchell 238256 from Bari to Capodichino airport in Naples. On the 22nd he travelled on Dakota 174289 to Cazes aerodrome in Casablanca via Maison Blanche in Algeria. On the 24th he boarded Liberator 439210 and was flown to RAF St. Mawgan near Newquay, and finally, on 25th June, he was flown on a Hudson to RAF Hendon in North London.

13

JAMES RADCLIFFE AND THE CITIZENS OF CIRCUMSTANCE

When Rudolph Stuppel was killed trying to save the wounded partisans, Jim Ratcliffe was severely injured, with multiple gunshots to the head, right leg and buttocks, and he was helped to escape to a farm in the hills. However, the farm came under attack and he was captured for the second time. He then spent six weeks in Belgrade under intensive interrogation by the Gestapo, during which time he lost four stone in weight, and all his teeth. Later, he was sent to Blechammer concentration camp as a slave labourer, then, after two months he was taken to Offizierslager 79 (Officers Camp 79), which had been established in December 1943 with men transferred from camps in Italy. Eventually, there was a community of 2500, or more, British officers gathered, not only from the United Kingdom, but also from Canada, Australia, New Zealand and South Africa. There were also Viceroy Commissioned officers from the Indian Army. A small contingent of other rank POWs acted as orderlies. The camp was at Waggum near Brunswick. It was located close to the autobahn, and to a small disused Luftwaffe airfield. It was housed in a three story brick building that had previously been the home of a German parachute regiment; this was surrounded by a barbed wire perimeter fence with watchtowers. The camp was in one of three woods that were about half a mile away from each other. In one of these, there was a Hermann Göring aircraft engine factory, where it was believed that the dreaded V1 and V2 'flying bombs' were made. On arrival, the men found that the guards at Oflag 79 were mostly elderly, and their clothes were of a poor quality. Most of them were unfit for active service because of age, or had been wounded. Some had very nasty frost bites from service in Russia, missing fingers and toes, and ears hidden beneath black patches.

Bob Parrott was recaptured during the same week as Jim Ratcliffe, towards the end of November 1943. However, he was initially sent to Oflag VIII-F. The camp at Mahrisch-Trubau contained around 2,000 officers, mostly British, captured in North Africa and the Greek Islands, but there were also a number of Greek, French and American POWs. Bob was in charge of a tunnel, which was discovered after three month's work. In July 1944 all the prisoners were transferred to Oflag 79. The Russians were advancing, so the men were put into cattle trucks for the three day journey to Brunswick.

Jim Ratcliffe was responsible to the Senior British Officer for the security of all secret equipment within the camp. There were three hidden radios from which the prisoners were kept informed of all the news broadcast on the BBC. One of these radios, nicknamed 'the Canary' had been constructed from all kinds of bits and pieces by a group of men while they were in another camp. Many of the parts were brought in by foreign workers, who were in and out of the camp every day, and somehow the men managed to transport this radio with them when they were moved to Oflag 79. Its normal home was behind a bookcase, which was attached to the wall in one of the huts, but it was hastily rehoused under the floorboards whenever the Germans commenced a search. On one occasion there was no time to hide the radio, but the searching Germans pulled everything apart except the bookcase, and the radio continued to play an essential role.

On 24th August 1944, during a daylight air raid, a number of high explosive, anti-personnel and incendiary bombs fell within the camp area. The B-24s of the USAAF 2nd Bomb Division had missed their target, which was the hidden factory in the next wood. The prisoner casualties included three killed, seven badly injured and thirty slightly wounded. There was a higher number of casualties among the Germans. Every building in the camp was damaged, one being rendered permanently uninhabitable. The cookhouse and the electric lighting system were destroyed. The water and drainage system was put out of action, except for two barracks, and large bomb craters appeared in the outdoor games area.

Some of the bombs that had fallen within the perimeter of the camp did not explode, and Jim Ratcliffe took it on himself to deal with them. Everyone else moved to a place of safety away from the area, and he set to work with the only tools he had to hand; nothing more than his personal cutlery set. He successfully made the bombs safe. The combination of his various actions led to the award of the DSO and the George Medal, Gazetted on 21st February 1946, in recognition of conspicuous gallantry in carrying out hazardous work, in a very brave manner, while a prisoner of war. However, a tragic event in Yugoslavia was possibly the reason why his name was not put forward for higher recognition. His Senior British Officer, during his time with the partisans, was Major Neville Darewski (aka Temple). On 12th November 1944 he was killed in a freak accident in the town of Marsaglia. A truck loaded with partisans approached, and Darewski stepped into the road and put his hand up for the truck to stop. The truck pulled up at the side of the road where there was no footpath, just a stone wall. Just as the Major stated to climb on board, the truck lurched forward and crushed him into the wall.

Life inside Oflag 79 became grim after the bombing. There was no light for ten days, no proper drainage for three weeks, and no heating for three months. It would be the beginning of December before the prisoners were able to have their first hot shower again. There was no hot food except German coffee, which was made from acorns and tasted vile. In spite of these discomforts, educational classes were increased, with about five hundred officers preparing for examinations. There were plenty of theatrical and musical events to help alleviate the dreadful conditions and the poor food. By the end of the year, the country was in such a state that no trains from Switzerland or lorries from Sweden could get through. Soon the number of Red Cross parcels dwindled, at first to one a fortnight, then to one a month, until they finally stopped completely.

Robert Parrott was fully occupied with the construction of an escape tunnel. The walls in the basement consisted of large stone blocks about two feet square, and a group of prisoners managed to lever two of the blocks out and started digging a tunnel. They were fortunate in that they were able to surreptitiously dispose of the earth into the bomb craters left by the Yanks. The men slept in two tier bunks, which had wooden slats, and these slats were needed to shore up the walls and sides of the tunnel. Slowly but surely, the slats were removed and stored in one of the huts until they were needed. In the meantime, the prisoners used all the saved string from the Red Cross parcels to replace the slats on their beds. In fact they found the string supports in their beds gave them a much more comfortable night's sleep. The digging of the tunnel took place through an appalling wet winter, and when they had dug themselves under the fencing, a whole section of the barbed wire fencing and the poles that supported it slowly subsided, leaning over at an angle of 45 degrees. They were all lined up for roll call at the time, and captors and captives alike watched, fascinated, as the twenty foot high fences collapsed.

The announcement that Robert Parrott had been awarded the Military Cross, in recognition of gallant and distinguished services in North Africa, was published in the London Gazette on 13th September 1945. This was followed by an announcement, on 1st November, that a Bar to the Military Cross had been awarded to him, in recognition of gallant and distinguished services in the field.

In early 1945, life for the prisoners was grim. The camp was overcrowded, the sanitation primitive, and the cold intense; above all, the inmates suffered from a gripping hunger. Rations dealt out to them were a bare minimum; a few boiled potatoes a day and a small piece of black bread once a week.

A group of Allied officers decided that one good thing should come out of the miserable squalor of their existence. They realised that the rather ordinary needs that they longed for were also denied to so many young boys back home, even in peacetime. The idea was to endow a boy's club in a UK city at the end of the war. On 14th February, a mass meeting of the POWs was held in a large attic, with bomb holes in the roof; an icy wind whistled through the spaces where the windows had been. The prisoners sat huddled in their blankets for warmth while the scheme was outlined to them. They listened to the chairman of the group, Lieutenant Colonel James Dunnill, explaining that it would be a challenge to the wasted months and years in captivity, and a memorial to comrades who had fallen.

Initially, the audience was not won over, but then a tough, six foot tall paratrooper got up and said that he was a cockney from a slum in the East End of London, and that as a youth, his boys' club had meant everything to him. A vote was taken, and the proposal was overwhelmingly accepted. A committee of trustees was elected, and the task of securing the support of those not present, raising the money, and, in due time, building the club had begun.

The committee produced a booklet with Red Cross materials. It was entitled *Citizens of Circumstance*, and the whole prison camp got behind the scheme with huge enthusiasm. There were concerts, plays, and raffles to raise money; artists painted pictures and sold them; hoarded cigarettes were sold. Cheques and bankers' orders were written on scraps of paper. Prizes underwritten by some of the POWs included a weekend for two at the Savoy, a year's subscription to *Punch*, and kippers from the Isle of Man.

After the war, it was decided that the club should be in London, and the London Federation of Boys Clubs suggested Fulham, which had no major boys' club to serve it. The centre of Fulham was a somewhat depressed area at the time, and had suffered substantial damage during the Blitz.

The Duke of Edinburgh officially opened the club on 11th July 1949. The original object of the trust was to 'promote the bodily, mental and spiritual welfare of boys in the United Kingdom, under the age of twenty one.' On 14th May 1997 the trust changed its name to The Brunswick Club Trust, and the object was amended to 'promote the development of boys and young men, and girls and young women, in achieving their full physical, intellectual, social and spiritual potential.'

Initially consisting of two Nissen huts, The Brunswick Boys Club has since been renamed The Brunswick Club for Young People, and is now a purpose-built youth centre offering a range of excellent facilities and services for the young people of Hammersmith & Fulham.

Oflag 79 camp was liberated by the US Ninth Army on 12th April 1945. On the same day in the United States, President Franklin D. Roosevelt suffered a massive stroke, and died in his home at Warm Springs in Georgia.

James Moore Ratcliffe was subsequently seconded to the BAOR as a War crimes investigator leading an SAS team. His German interpreter at that time became his wife.

14

PICKING UP THE PIECES
AND MAKING A NEW LIFE

John returned to England, after over two years away, to a home life where just about everything had changed. He travelled to stay with his parents, in their retirement home in East Meon, and tried to readjust to all the changes which had taken place during his long absence but he was at a bit of a low ebb. One evening, he was driving in the rain on his way to nearby Petersfield, when he saw a young lady waiting for a bus and getting very wet. Ever the gentleman, he pulled up and offered her a lift.

Nineteen year old Barbara Phelps had recently moved to the area from London with her family. She was working in the part of the Admiralty that had moved to Aldworth House in Hazelmere. This beautiful property with extensive grounds had been built for the Poet Laureate Alfred Lord Tennyson, but now the grounds were filled with Nissen huts where the Admiralty employees worked. They were expected to take their turn to volunteer for firefighting duty, watching out for incendiary bombs, and then dousing any subsequent fires with buckets of water. Barbara was heading from her home to catch a train to take her from Petersfield to Hazlemere.

A few days later, they met again, this time while queuing to use the telephone box in the village. Always conscious of the correct social norms, John asked Barbara to walk with him to his parents' house so that they could all be properly introduced.

Barbara told him about a dance that was due to take place in the village hall, and that was the start of their romance.

After three weeks, John was back on duty. He undertook a twin-engine refresher course before being posted to No. 1 Ferry Unit in Pershore, to collect new aircraft from the factories, and fly them to destinations in Europe, West Africa and Egypt, as replacements for war damaged aircraft.

As if everything that had happened to John and the news of the loss of so many of his comrades was not enough, the worst was yet to come. Micky Carmichael had been repatriated and eventually arrived home in Chalfont St. Giles on 3rd June 1944. He sent a telegram to his younger brother, Squadron Leader John William Carmichael DFC, to tell him that he would visit soon. On the night of 13th June, John Carmichael and his crew were in their Liberator, taking part in Coastal Command Operations off Brittany, but they failed to return and were later officially presumed killed.

Determined to get back to operational flying at the earliest opportunity, Micky signed up for a refresher flying course at Booker during his month long repatriation leave. In November 1944, John and Micky were gazetted MBE for distinguished service. This was for valuable information, of a secret nature, acquired during their escape, specifically the details of the Military Installation at Macerata.

On 31st December 1944, at the age of 27, Micky took off from Brize Norton. He was taking part in a formation flying exercise on Nettleton Top, Lincolnshire at the controls of Spitfire EN681. Just a few seconds after a radio communication with his leader, his aircraft left the formation and flew out of control until it hit the ground at 10:15. The assumption was that he had lost consciousness, but the cause of this was never determined.

In August 1944, John Mott had been recommended for the Military Cross; this did not come to fruition, and there are a number of possible explanations for this. There had already been some awards of the MC to airmen in recognition of their actions on the ground. Such awards required the endorsement of a senior officer, with firsthand knowledge of the events in question; it was often the case that the recommendation faltered at this hurdle. However, long after the war, Mervyn repeated the gist of a conversation that had taken place with John, when it was made clear that he would not accept any award that was not also available to Micky Carmichael. It was only many decades later that it became possible for the MC to be awarded posthumously.

John was determinedly trying to find out the fate of his helpers in France. Ever since he had been made aware of the dossier containing details of his activities with the Resistance in Nantes, he had been fearful of what might have befallen them. This proved to be an uphill task.

In the meantime, on one of John's trips to Cairo, he met his ex-fiancée. Whynifred Bignall who had enlisted some time before, and was now stationed there. This was the last time they had any contact, though she did occasionally keep in touch with Mervyn and Frances on her return to England after the end of the war.

Back in England, Barbara was helping John to pick up the threads of normal life, and their romance flourished. On a later trip to Cairo, he purchased a wedding ring for Barbara, and he was able to organise bananas from Cairo for all the guests, at the wedding breakfast, after their snowy wedding on 27th January 1945. The bananas were a particular treat because their import had been banned by the Ministry of Food in November 1940. A much treasured wedding gift was a pair of silver napkin rings from Micky Carmichael's parents.

BROTHERS BRIEFLY REUNITED WHEN MERVYN WAS
FLOWN HOME ON COMPASSIONATE LEAVE FOR THE BIRTH OF HIS
FOURTH CHILD AND PIP WAS ON 60 DAYS' LEAVE BEFORE HEADING TO INDIA.
MOTT FAMILY COLLECTION

The end of the war in Europe triggered a search for the identities of the hundreds of helpers, so that they could receive some level of compensation, and awards for gallantry where appropriate. This work commenced within IS9, and over the next two years, 35,000 claims in Western Europe had been processed. There were many bogus claims, a number of exaggerated claims, and many more helpers who never came forward.

The planned certificate of thanks for the helpers was not carried through in its original form. Winston Churchill agreed to sign each one, but the RAF insisted that an airman should sign the certificates awarded for helping escaping and evading airmen. It was then agreed that Air Chief Marshall Sir Arthur Tedder would sign these certificates. Unfortunately, the signature used was a rubber stamp which made them less meaningful.

Far more significant was the founding of the Royal Air Forces Escaping Society in 1945. The RAF funded this, and almost 3,000 successful evaders were canvassed to join. Initially 800 signed up, and it seems likely that many evaders did not realise that it was intended to be a charitable organisation and not just an old boys' club. It was formed to provide help to those in the former occupied countries in WW2 who had put their lives at risk to assist and save members of the Royal Air Forces (that is, Air Forces of the British Commonwealth) who were attempting to escape and evade capture. It helped the widows, dependents and orphans of those who died and those requiring medical treatment or otherwise in need. It also fostered continued friendship between escapers and evaders and their helpers. Air Chief Marshal Sir Basil Embry was the president of the RAFES from its formation until the 1970s.

The society was based at the Duke of York's Headquarters, London, and had the Latin motto *solvitur ambulando*. This motto goes far back in time when it was reputably interpreted as 'check your calculation by measurement' (pace it out). Over time, it was used to suggest that there might come a time when, instead of continuing to pore over books, some gentle exercise might help to solve the problem. By the time it was adopted by the Royal Air Forces Escaping Society, the literal translation of 'Solved by walking' became more loosely translated as 'Saved by walking'.

On 5th May 1946, shortly after the birth of his daughter Virginia, John wrote to the secretary of RAFES at the Air Ministry, Room 475, Adastral House, Kingsway. He requested the gen on the RAFES as mentioned in the journal and gave details of his evasion and escape. The response was sent to him at Pershore, and explained that a letter and a reminder had been sent to John at RAF Credenhill, which was the address they had obtained from Officers' Records. They enclosed the required pro forma and requested the subscription for 1946.

On 11th January 1947, John wrote to apologise for the fact that he had been unable to provide addresses for all his helpers. Like the other evaders and escapers he avoided noting any details about these extraordinary, brave people during his journey to freedom; they would have been put at great risk should their activities have come to light during the war. It was very difficult to establish the details retrospectively, but John wrote to say that Mme. Delavigne might be able to help him to find them during his planned visit to Brittany at the end of the month. In the same letter, he asked for assistance with obtaining a new passport. He was now living with his wife and baby at RAF Pershore, but his passport, along with all his private papers and furniture, were currently in storage and not accessible. His passport had expired in 1945, and a new passport could only be issued when this one was surrendered. A request was sent on his behalf to the individual responsible at the military permit section of the Passport Office, and he was able to make the trip to France with his wife and baby.

Tantine was still far from well and required help with the simplest tasks such as dressing and undressing. Barbara and John did their best to cope, but then the baby fell ill and the house was very cold. When they had to return home, it was in the knowledge that Tantine would need continued help for the foreseeable future.

John wrote again to the Secretary of the RAFES on 9th April, regarding a letter he had received from one of his helpers in response to some information that had been sent to him. This was certainly one of the exaggerated claims that formed part of the thousands of claims that were made. John had listed Mr Arnošt Polák as a Czech from Prague: 'Mr Polák was a Czech who had rented a house in Italy after escaping from a political prison in Italy. He was making his way back to Czechoslovakia and he gave me shelter for a day'. In November 1945 Arnošt Polák wrote a very long letter to John, care of his father. Quite rightly, he listed all the servicemen he had sheltered, but then he wrote a vast screed about all his valiant deeds fighting with the partisans and volunteering/serving with the 8th Army, the 50th British Brigade, 352 British Royal Artillery, The Canadian Westminster Regiment, twice at the New Zealander Forces, the Engineer Unit, the Divisions Supply and the 6th NZ Brigade, and finally the Polish Forces. He then pointed out that many Italians requested awards and got them.

Believing deeply that he had missed out on decorations for his valour, he wrote;

'So I believe I had a claim for the 8th Army Cross and some other distinctions. I am ashamed seeing many of my friends and fellows, wearing British and American distinctions, and being sure they did not serve the common cause in the manner that I did. So I believed you perhaps have more connection with the proper authorities to do something for me in this direction and I would be very grateful to you…'

The letter that John sent with this report stated:

'The attached letter I received from the Czech gentleman quite amused me. I cannot guarantee the truth of it, except that he certainly welcomed F/L Carmichael, Capt. Neill and myself when we reached his abode. We only stayed for one night though, so what his attitude was, in the event of an antici-pated stay, I cannot say. Perhaps however, you could pass the letter on through the proper channels'.

John's letter continued with many details of the situation with regard to Mme. Delavigne, in which John stressed the work she had done and what she had been forced to endure as a result. There is no doubt that John was dedicated to helping her in every way possible.

At the beginning of July, John was informed by the RAFES that they had received a reply from the Allied Screening Commission in Italy with regard to Arnošt Polák, he had already been awarded the diploma of thanks, signed by Field Marshal Lord Alexander, and the commission did not consider that his assistance to Allied personnel warranted any higher award.

15

JOHN MOTT, A FAMILY MAN

In July 1947, John spent six weeks with the London University Air Squadron. Richard Adrian John Mott was born on 3rd August, in Evesham in Worcestershire, and the following month John took up the post of Chief Instructor at RAF Titchfield in Hampshire and the family moved to Petersfield.

Not long afterwards, on 1st September, Pip Mott was present when the British flag was pulled down in India, and after a ghastly, dangerous journey across India to Bombay, he continued to Port Said and boarded RMS The Empress of Scotland which arrived in Liverpool on 6th October. He moved to Rushes House in Petersfield, together with his wife and daughter and finally Arthur and Florence had two of their sons and some of their grandchildren very close by, with Mervyn, Frances and the rest of their grandchildren just fifty miles away.

In November 1947, John purchased a helpers' badge from the RAFES (Royal Airforces Escaping Society). Tantine treasured this and stored it in a silk grosgrain lined briefcase with all the miniatures of the many awards bestowed on her and Adrien during the two world wars. In December, John submitted a translated report of the assistance given to Allied airmen by Monsieur and Madame Delavigne, together with some more detailed facts that had not appeared in the report itself. He felt very strongly that Tantine had not been given the recognition she deserved, and he did his very best to rectify this.

RAFES PIN
COURTESY OF
CHRISTINE PARK

John's attempts to garner greater recognition for Mme. Delavigne met something of a brick wall, and he was informed that, 'As far as Western Europe is concerned, generally, the work of the various Awards Bureaux was finished in the latter half of 1946, when the outstanding claims for recognition submitted by helpers was cleared up, the staffs disbanded and the records placed in safe custody'.

It is easy to see just how important the work of the RAFES was to become over the following decades. Like all the other members, John worked tirelessly to raise funds, and to help in every way possible to improve the lives of the helpers and their families. In due course he became a trustee of the fund.

In August 1949, the next major event for the Mott family involved arranging for Tantine to visit England, so that John's parents and grandmother could thank her in person. Initially, the secretary of RAFES was unable to book a ticket for her travel, but John stepped in and booked for her to travel in First Class, from St. Malo to Southampton. Arthur sent copies of the photograph taken on an afternoon at Highlands in East Meon to members of the Mott family all over the globe. By this time, Tantine was in good health; the only visible reminder of what she had endured was that her hair remained very thin for the rest of her life. Before long, she became active in the care of the families of those members of the Resistance who had lost their lives during the war. She remained at the forefront of the work until just a couple of years before her death.

On 1st October 1945, l'Amicale des Déportés Politiques de la Résistance de Mauthausen et de ses Kommandos Dépendants was founded. The original members were particularly survivors of KZ Mauthausen-Gusen and its subcamps. The Amicale de Mauthausen unearthed the fact that 198,000 people of 25 different nationalities (10,000 of them French) were deported to KZ Mauthausen. 118,000 people died from forced labour, or in one of the gas chambers, which were installed inside the camp. In the postwar years, the Amicale helped families of the missing or their children.

At the 1977 tribunal in Grenoble, the remaining members of the 'old guard' handed over the continuation of their work to the next generation. A photograph was published in a French newspaper article with a caption that translates as: 'At the tribunal during the Grenoble Congress, in 1977, Mme. Delavigne is between R.P. Riquet and our departed comrade Sugranes. Joséphine Delavigne, a resistance deportee to Ravensbruch and Mauthausen 1509, along with her husband, Adrien Delavigne who died at Gusen 60137. Mme. Delavigne was the Vice President of our society and the doyen of our deported comrades.'

De nos camarades :   Photo Murawa

A la tribune, au congrès de Grenoble en 1977,
Mme Delavigne entre le R.-P. Riquet et notre
regretté camarade Sugranes.

My first memories of my Uncle John are of holiday times and family celebrations. He was always kind and had a gift for seeing the bright side of each day. On one particular day, John, Barbara and my two cousins had called in to see my parents, only to find that my youngest sister Elizabeth had just arrived into the world; John decided to collect the rest of the children from school and bring us home to meet the baby.

As I grew older, and began to take an interest in books and films about the war, he always reminded me to think of the unsung heroes, and not just the men who were at the heart of these adventure stories. He was quite determined that he didn't want his own story to be the subject of a book, adding that he certainly did not wish to bring the darker side of his individual war into the family home.

Family life was of prime importance to John, and bringing Tantine to East Meon to meet his parents and grandmother (Gran Gran), in 1949, was a very special event. Tantine never learnt to speak any English, but John was always able to translate for her. For the rest of her life, his family were her family, and he and my aunt supported her in every way that they could.

TANTINE'S VISIT TO EAST MEON – MOTT FAMILY COLLECTION

My earliest memories of East Meon are of two photographs on the mantelpiece; one of the three brothers in uniform at the end of the war, and one of Uncle John, also in uniform, but with embroidered RAF wings under the glass. I loved hearing the story of how Prince Rainier provided the needles and silks for John to make the wings, while he was imprisoned in a fort. My grandmother was very patient when she was asked, again and again, about the silver brooch she always wore on the lapel of her coat.

On 29th June 1951, John was promoted to Squadron Leader. He was deeply involved with the planning for the Coronation Review of the RAF, at Odiham, on 15th July 1953, when the Queen and Prince Philip reviewed the Royal Air Force. He was at the heart of a team, who worked long hours working out the complexities of this huge operation, and it's hard to imagine, now, how any project of this magnitude could be brought to fruition without the use of computers.

During the previous month, the units had relocated to the airfields from which they were to operate on the day. The routes and timing over Odiham were complex; there were to be just 30 seconds between formations. The bombers and Coastal Command aircraft had 45 seconds. Most of the navigation was reliant on a stopwatch and a map. John and his team had undergone a formation practice for the newsreel early on the day. When it came to the review flypast itself, the majority of the flypast was achieved within five seconds of the target. Rehearsals had taken place in difficult and cloudy conditions, and were fraught with danger, but the weather was kind for the review itself. John was at the controls of Vickers 668 Varsity WF387 leading Formation 10, operating from Thorney Island. Their time over Odiham was 15:44; Altitude 1,100 feet; Speed 166mph/145 knots.

The following day the Air Officer commanding No. 11 Group sent a telegram to the personnel involved, it read: 'MAGNIFICENT SHOW (.) WELL DONE (.)'

In 1953, television was for the privileged few. Together with my brothers and sisters, I had watched the Coronation, and had a wonderful indoor picnic with friends of the family, while my parents were able to enjoy the procession as guests at the Foreign Office, overlooking the processional route, as my mother was working there at the time. On 11th July, the day that the RAF Coronation Review was held at RAF Odiham, I was sitting in the classroom watching the flypast on a small black and white television screen. Peter Dimmock was describing the action, when I suddenly heard him talking about my Uncle John; I was so very proud, especially when the teacher asked me about him in front of the whole class.

VARSITY WF387
ARTWORK BY GEOFF PLEASANCE

In August 1958, John and Barbara's second daughter, Suzannah, was born. John was posted to a staff appointment at Headquarters Home Command in 1959, until his retirement from the RAF. On leaving, he took the civil service exams and began a new career as a tax inspector. Kristina, their third daughter, was born in 1964, and around that time John and his brothers became concerned about their father's health. Arthur, restless after the death of his wife, had travelled to spend time with his brother-in-law in South Africa. He lived for a while with Mervyn's family but, when they moved to Northern Ireland, Arthur went to live with Pip and his family, before deciding to return to the Bournemouth area where he met and married his second wife. The wedding, in 1962, brought a number of the Mott family together; I was a student nurse at Saint Bartholomew's Hospital, and was begrudgingly allowed to swop my day off to attend my grandfather's wedding. The rest of my family were in Northern Ireland at the time. Grandpa soon became very frail, and the brothers became concerned about the fact that none of the families lived nearby. This was the trigger that instigated a move back to Petersfield for John and Barbara, allowing them to be near enough to keep an eye on Arthur's welfare.

Meanwhile, Virginia and Richard followed in their father's footsteps and joined the WRAF and RAF, respectively. He was very proud of this, and in a letter to a family member, John wrote: 'Richard is commissioned in the RAF, after graduating from Cranwell, where he won the trophy for applied flying on his course – I think that is the best prize he could have, even better than the sword of honour, as it shows that he was outstanding as a pilot throughout his two and a half years on the course'.

In his own words, John had 'changed sides', and now worked with Grant Thornton Consultancy. In 1971, Richard married Diana Easlea in a beautiful wedding in Winchester. Tantine sent an unusual gift of some impeccably monogrammed linen that had been embroidered locally in Lesconil. Five years later, John and Barbara were delighted to become grandparents with the birth of Andrew in 1976, and Louisa was born in 1978.

My own wedding, in April 1976, gave me a chance to catch up with my uncles and aunts during a brief visit home from South Africa. This trip probably sowed the seeds that led to our permanent move back to England at the start of the following year. In 1977, the Queen's Silver Jubilee was marked with a review of the RAF at RAF Finningley, Yorkshire. Sitting with my baby son, I watched the flypast on a colour television. This time, it was Raymond Baxter who was commentating when twenty two Jet Provosts in the shape of a number 25 flew overhead. Flight Lieutenant Richard Mott was at the controls of the lead aircraft on the curve of the number two in the formation, and Raymond Baxter outlined Richard's father's role in the Coronation Review flypast to the watching public.

Barbara's mother and Tantine both died in 1980, and Tantine left her house in Lesconil to John. John and Barbara planned a trip to Lesconil to sort out the house that Tantine had left to them, and to tidy up her affairs. Their son-in-law, Brigadier Richard Dennis OBE, recounts the story here:

'In the summer of 1980, some 5 years after we met and two years before we were to be married, my then girlfriend, Susie Mott, invited me to join her and her parents at their house in Lesconil – Ty An Avel – for a week or two. At the time I was stationed in Munster, Northern Germany, some 1200 kms and a 12 hour drive from Lesconil. But I was young, in love – and the petrol was, in those days, duty free, at least for the German leg of the journey! And Susie was to have the house to herself for two days before her parents arrived.

I duly set out one Friday morning for the long drive into the arms of my beloved, arriving late that evening, tired but happy as I was welcomed by Susie and set eyes on Lesconil for the first time in the gathering dusk of a July evening.

The following morning, I set out on foot in to the village to buy some bread and croissants for breakfast. I found the boulangerie – set back some 100 m from the port without any great difficulty and in what was then fairly rudimentary school boy French asked, not unreasonably, for 'une baguette, deux croissants, s'il vous plais'. What happened next still remains a little confused in my mind even to this day. Firstly, instead of simply being given my bread and croissants I received a short sharp inquiry from the baker's wife in what sounded remarkably like Welsh (but which I now know to be Breton) asking me if I wanted my bread with or without salt. Secondly, I slipped in to what was for me the most natural foreign language at the time – German. And thirdly I very quickly found myself standing outside on the pavement having been refused service and with some very dirty looks following me out of the shop. Somewhat perplexed I made my way back up to the house where the object of my affections asked, not unreasonably, where breakfast was. I duly explained that there had been some sort of misunderstanding at the bakery and I didn't have any so it was decided that I had better get back into my car, drive the 3 km to the next nearest boulangerie in Plobbanalec and try my luck there. This I duly did and, being careful to keep my mouth firmly shut and make my order known largely through grunting and pointing I was soon safely on my way back with a Renault 5 awash with the fragrance of fresh bread and croissants.

By the time I turned back in to the driveway of the house no more than 30 minutes can have elapsed since the original incident at the Lesconil boulangerie – but that was ample time for the great and the good of the village to mobilise. For there, on the door step, clutching her dressing gown around her, was Susie surrounded by a small posse consisting of the priest, the mayor and two of the Sisters of Mercy demanding to know what she thought she was playing at as the daughter of "Le Commandant" as I discovered they referred to Susie's father bringing a German into the village. "Tu a mariee un Boche" I remember them saying with much finger wagging – completely oblivious to the fact that I wasn't German – and we certainly weren't married!

Thankfully the posse dispersed as I arrived – with yet more dirty looks – and the truth and the enormity of what I had unwittingly managed to do slowly began to dawn on me. Lesconil – a village with a very proud and terrible reputation as a hot bed of the Resistance to the Nazi occupation, a reputation which prompted the occupiers to execute the sons of nine of the most prominent families in the village in June 1944. Lesconil – a village which revered Susie's father as a hero of the wider Resistance effort and who they had taken into their hearts over the years since the war that he had been a regular visitor there to see Mme. Delavigne. Lesconil – now subjected to a blonde haired, blue eyed stranger speaking German in the boulangerie and apparently cohabiting with Le Commandant's daughter. Quell horreur!

Having pieced this jigsaw together in my mind I took a deep breath, a pocket full of loose change and made a bee line for the call box in the square to report my faux pas to Susie's father who was due to sail that night and join us the following day. Needless to say he found the whole episode quite hilarious but he undertook to do some repair work on my behalf and sure enough by the time he and Mrs Mott arrived the following day a council of elders had been convened in the Hotel du Port that evening and I was duly introduced as a British officer, defender of the Faith and an all round good bloke to name but three and the wine flowed and all was forgiven.

But the story doesn't quite end there: for many years after that, until his death in the early 90s, Monsieur Manis, the priest, would insist on stopping and clicking his heels together in a mock Nazi salute every time we met in the village – something which he found absolutely hilarious and which to this day reminds me of that first, memorable visit to Lesconil.'

THE HOUSE – COURTESY OF ANDREW MOTT

16

PER ARDUA AD ASTRA

There are simply no words to express the shock of the phone call, from my mother, to tell me that Richard had died in Germany. I learned the stark facts later. On 11th July 1980 Richard was at the controls of his RAF Phantom XV418 when it took off from the RAF military airbase at Wildenrath. The aircraft crashed in farmland at Lohne, near Diepholz, Lower Saxony, during an attempted 270 degree aileron roll manoeuvre, which was being filmed automatically from the brake parachute compartment of a lead aircraft of the same type. The filming was for a BBC *Man Alive* documentary about low level NATO flying in the Federal Republic of Germany. The pilot and navigator (Flight Lieutenant Richard Adrian John Mott and Flight Lieutenant Ian Michael Johnson) were both killed.

All these years later, and with Andrew Mott's permission, I quote from his Facebook status on 15th March 2016: 'Thanks for all my birthday wishes. I'm actually happy to make 40 and be happy, healthy, busy and (occasionally) useful! My father did not make his 34th birthday, so I am very thankful for my good fortune today.' Just two weeks earlier, I had met up with Louisa, at Kristina's wedding, and I know just how proud Richard would have been to see her now.

There are some lovely earlier memories of the Mott families coming together for the weddings of Susie and Jinny, and the golden wedding party for Mervyn and Frances, followed a few years later by one for John and Barbara.

When John retired, he set up his own business advising individuals on their tax affairs. Our family move to Odiham, and the purchase of a small business brought us back into close contact. Our meetings with John always took place in Odiham, giving my husband, Andrew, time to get home from work, and giving me time to tuck the children into bed. We always endeavoured to have the paperwork in good shape so that we could hand it over without much need for discussion, then we would relax and catch up on family matters. It so happened that John and I each bought an Amstrad computer, and entered the new world of word processing. With both children at school, I embarked on a year's training at college, and once again I broached the subject of writing a book about John's evasion and escape. This time he gave me permission to go ahead, but only after his death, and on the condition that I included some of his brave contemporaries whose deeds deserved to be recognised. John's knowledge of agents being trained on the airfield in WW2 intrigued me, when we had discussions about Odiham.

FRANCO-BELGE AIR TRAINING SCHOOL
RAF ODIHAM 1940 – COURTESY OF JOEL DIGGLE

In 1925, the airfield at Odiham was established as a summer camp for army cooperation aircraft, utilising a grass runway. The airfield was part of the common fields situated
south of the High Street and west of Long Lane. These were called Snatchanger and
Buryfields and were used for grazing by those residents of Odiham who had commoners'
rights. Between October and March, the land reverted to grazing land for cattle and
sheep. Eventually, the area became a permanent airfield and the only signs of its recent
usage were a few farm buildings in the corner of the Snatchanger field.

In 1940, the Franco-Belge Air Training School (Elementary Flying Training School)
was set up at Odiham. General de Gaulle first saw the Cross of Lorraine emblazoned
on the French Tricoleur, while inspecting the 300 French pilots here in July. Although
angered by it at first, he soon saw its value as a symbol of resistance, owing to its association with Joan of Ark. The Cross then became the official trademark of the Free
French. On 16th August, Yeo Thomas, later best remembered as 'The White Rabbit',
was sent here to become one of the interpreters assigned to assist the evacuated French
Air Force personnel. He later joined the SOE, where, known under a variety of names,
he was flown into occupied France three times, before being captured and tortured
by the Gestapo. On his return from Buchenwald concentration camp, he visited the
Peskett family who were living in a house called Three Ways in Odiham where he had
been billeted; before leaving he signed the visitors' book.

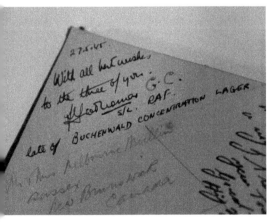 

YEO THOMAS RETURNS TO ODIHAM (COURTESY OF JAMES PESKETT)

Raymond Fassin was another heroic agent who came to the Franco-Belge Air Training
School and was based in Tours as an air observer at the time when Petain signed the
armistice. He travelled to England on the Polish ship *John Sobieski* on 21st June 1940.

Two days later, he signed an employment contract with the Air Force of Free France (FAFL). On completion of his training in Odiham, he was assigned to the Free French air staff. He underwent months of training before joining an organisation which became the Bureau Central de Renseignements et d'Action (BCRA). Together with Jean Moulin, he parachuted into France from an RAF 138 Squadron Special Duties Whitley, for the first time on 1st January 1942. His last journey to France was on 15th September 1943, when he parachuted from an RAF 138 SD Squadron Halifax, and his valuable work came to an end when he was arrested in April 1944. Raymond Fassin died as a result of ill-treatment on 12th February 1945. In recognition of his valuable work, he became a Chevalier (Knight) of the Légion d'honneur, whilst in captivity, in August 1944.

When I first moved to Odiham, thirty five years ago, my uncle told me that he had been involved in the training of French SOE agents in Snatchanger's barn, on the perimeter of the airfield. It was just after he completed his Lysander training with the Special Duties Squadron, and after his year long evasion. Speaking fluent French, his recent experiences were considered to be of valuable assistance in communicating with the agents, and instructing them on the requirements for Lysander pick-up operations. Although he was never one to recount much of his wartime story, he did say that the initial parachute training for these agents consisted of instructors talking the agents through the required procedures, as they sat on a beam, high in the barn. There is no record of any of the SD aeroplanes flying into Odiham so he presumably made the journey from Tempsford by road and train.

Verifying the fact that French agents were trained here in Odiham was a long, and seemingly fruitless, search, and then I struck gold. With the kind permission of the publisher, the following is an extract from Bill Randle's autobiography *Blue Skies and Dark Nights*:

'During World War 2, Odiham had been used as a briefing centre for SOE agents who were then either flown across the Channel from Tangmere in Lysanders or dropped by parachute in France. This activity was cloaked in secrecy and the briefing done in the oddly named Snatchanger's Barn on the south side of the airfield. I was still a committee member of the Royal Air Forces Escaping Society and the Chairman, Olive Philpott MC, of Wooden Horse fame asked if I would host a party of some thirty French SOE operators, many of whom had passed through Odiham more than twenty years earlier.

With the full backing of 38 Group, we were able to treat the French veterans right royally; each had a host, many of whom could speak French. The station was toured and they then witnessed a good flying display which included many different types of aircraft, including a Spitfire and a Hurricane. They were taken to the now derelict Snatchanger's Barn and then flown around Hampshire in an Argosy. As they left the station to return to London, a Wessex flew alongside their coach trailing the French Tricolour.'

I was always curious about the details of John's life during the war, and occasionally he would refer to the specifics of his experiences. This fascinated me, but I knew better than to push for details. For example, when it came to the subject of interrogation and the grim circumstances of being thrown into a prison cell, two instances are clear in my mind.

In January 1991 a British Tornado bomber, crewed by John Peters and John Nichol, was shot down over Iraqi territory, and the two men were captured. After a number of days of mental and physical torture, they were forcibly shown on Iraqi television, and these pictures were then beamed across the world on every news broadcast. The evening that they were shown on British television, we were due to have a meeting with John. He phoned to postpone the meeting, explaining that he intended to call on John Peters's parents in Petersfield. He said that only someone who had been interrogated for days on end, by a determined enemy, could help them to understand the circumstances under which their son had spoken the words, provided by his captors.

Four years later, John was in hospital for major heart surgery. When I visited, and met other family members by his bedside, he was agitated, because every time he opened his eyes he could see a brick wall almost immediately outside the barred window of his room. As soon as the wonderful staff at the hospital became aware of the problem, he was moved to a ground floor room with a view of the garden through the French windows. On my second visit he assured me that he would definitely be at my father's 80th birthday party, which was due to take place just a few weeks later. True to his word, and probably not with medical approval, he proposed the toast, and the three brothers entertained a large gathering of family and friends with reminiscences about their childhood.

In the interim I had enjoyed a very special 'Old Blues Day' with the three brothers at Christ's Hospital, where Richard's son, Andrew, was a pupil.

THREE BROTHERS VISITING ANDREW MOTT ON OLD BLUES DAY
AUTHOR'S COLLECTION

Sir Barnes Wallace was an 'Old Blue' who had been involved in the development of the R100 airship. During the war, he invented the bouncing bomb used on the Dambuster raid in May 1943. In spite of the success of the raid, Barnes Wallace felt a high degree of responsibility for the huge loss of human life. After the war he was awarded £10,000 for the invention, but he had no wish to accept it and decided to give it to charity. Together with the RAF Benevolent Fund, a special bursary was created to pay for children of RAF personnel killed in service to attend Christ's Hospital for the duration of their school career. Andrew was a proud recipient of this bursary.

BARNES WALLACE CH PLATE – COURTESY OF ANDREW MOTT

In 1993, John spoke about evasion and escape in a lecture at the University Air Squadron in which he said:

'During the war I had three or four potentially terminal episodes, I can say that from my experiences evading before capture is far less stressful and far less difficult than trying to escape from captivity. When you first land behind enemy lines, particularly if you are uninjured, you are in a similar position to the locals apart from your uniform and your knowledge of the language you might well pass as one of them and, with their help, you may well return to your unit in a short space of time provided that you use your head, think fast and move away from your landing craft as quickly as possible.

Escape is far more problematic, from the moment of your capture you are known to your capturers, they know all about you, they know what you look like, they know how are dressed, they know how you walk, upright or stooping, they know if you are fit or injured, they know that your morale is very low and they know that you are disorientated, hungry and miserable. It takes you quite a while to recover, by which time it has got worse, until you reach the prison camp at which time they will probably take your photograph when you then realise the enormity of the situation you are in.

Remember that your instructions if captured are to give only your name rank and number, not an easy thing when you are being pushed around and shouted at and generally manhandled I can vouch for that.'

John somehow managed to see a particular quality in every day; he once delayed a journey with my children because it was raining. He looked knowingly at the sky and suggested that we should have a cup of tea before setting out. We started the journey in beautiful sunshine, and somewhere on the Alton Road, he pulled over and suggested a walk as he wanted to show us something. The children had short legs, and the grass was pretty wet, but we followed John into a clearing in the trees. The sun was shining through the wet leaves and there was a carpet of bluebells stretching as far as the eye could see.

On another occasion, he was travelling with his daughter, Jinny, and she felt he was being far too reasonable about some difficult traffic conditions; she eventually complained about his eternal optimism. He quietly told her that when you have been made to dig your own grave, and stand in front of it about be shot by a machine gun, only to be saved by the lunch bell, you are entitled to be an optimist.

In due course, four more grandsons had been born, and John and Barbara relished being grandparents.

Through all this time, often accompanied by his daughter Kristina, John continued to give talks about his evasion and escape on behalf of the RAFES. Fortunately, two of these talks were taped, and I have been able to obtain digitised versions of these, which have helped me enormously in my research.

In 2001, Andrew and I celebrated our silver wedding anniversary. My parents delighted us with a gift of the silver tea service that Uncle John had given them at the time of their own wedding. Sadly, that same year Pip, the youngest of the three brothers died, and the families came together for his funeral. Little did we know that John would only survive him by a few months. Uncle John's funeral took place on 21st May 2002 in the beautiful old church of Saint Mary Magdalen in Sheet. This was the church where he had played an active part on the PCC, but the congregation on that day came from far and wide. The church was full to overflowing, and the tributes and readings were heartfelt. As we were leaving the church, the organist, on impulse, broke into the theme tune from *The Dam Busters*. It was a clear spring day and the RAF bugler played *The Last Post* as the coffin was placed in the hearse. As if on cue, just as the last notes died away, from far up in the sky, we heard the sound of a propeller driven aircraft, and we all stood still and listened until the sky became quiet.

A poignant tribute to a true hero; Squadron Leader John Mott MBE, MiD, AE, RAF retd.

POSTSCRIPT

THE FORT DE LA REVÈRE 2015, COURTESY OF ANDREW MOTT

Andrew Mott wrote the following, at my request, to show how the family still keeps the memory of John's extraordinary story alive:

'We were holidaying in the South of France, just inland from Nice, at the end of the summer 2015. We are active holidaymakers who like to explore the areas where we stay, and hence we found ourselves in a pretty hill top village named Eze, which lies between Nice and Monte Carlo. The highlights of Eze are the beautiful exotic gardens and the castle ruins within. We were admiring the views, and reading the information plaques, when we noted one pointing out the Fort de la Revère, high above us. That name rang a bell, and after a minute or two I recalled that it was a camp in which my grandfather was detained, for a time, during the war. I also remembered the black and white pictures of the fort from my son's homework project, entitled Family History, which he had completed the year before.

So, once we had completed our trip to Eze, we decided to drive up to the fort to see what we might be able to see. Hence we drove up to the Grand Corniche, and then still further uphill to the Fort de la Revère, which is a military base with lots of open space enjoyed by hikers and dog walkers. The views are spectacular all along the beautiful coastline.

All of us, including my sons, recognised the outside area, from the old photos of where the prisoners were able to exercise. We walked most of the way around the fort, on the outside of the dry moat. The buildings inside the moat area were locked and gated, though in a state of disrepair. We saw a uniformed man inside.

It was an unexpected and memorable day for us, and I found it a real privilege to be there, and especially to be able to show Daniel and Oliver, his great grandsons, where he had been and to talk about him with them. We all found it hard to comprehend, and particularly how far it was above the sea where they were taken on occasion to wash and bathe.'

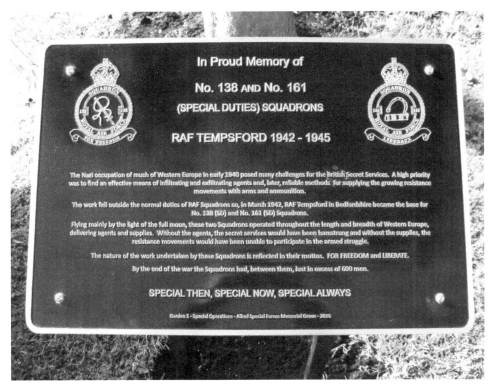

THE TEMPSFORD VETERANS AND RELATIVES ASSOCIATION (TVARA) PLAQUE TO THE TEMPSFORD SPECIAL DUTIES SQUADRONS WAS UNVEILED ON SUNDAY 11TH SEPTEMBER 2016 IN THE SPECIAL FORCES MEMORIAL GROVE AT THE NATIONAL MEMORIAL ARBORETUM, COURTESY OF BOB BODY

BIBLIOGRAPHY

BOOKS

Airborne Espionage: International Special Duties Operations in the World Wars, David Oliver, Sutton Publishing Ltd.

All Hell Let Loose, The World at War 1939-1945, Max Hastings, Harper Press

Black Lysander, Wing Commander John Nesbitt-Dufort, Jarrolds Publishers (London) Ltd.

Blue Skies and Dark Nights: The Autobiography of an Airman, Bill Randle, Peter Osborne Independent Books

Bravest of the Brave: The True Story of Wing Commander 'Tommy' Yeo Thomas, Mark Seaman, Michael O'Mara Books Ltd.

Committed To Escape: A New Zealand Soldier's Story, Daniel Johnston Riddiford M.C., Ruamahanga Press

Conscript Heroes, Peter Scott James, Edited by Keith James, Empire Publishing Service

Cruel Crossing, Escaping Hitler: Across the Pyrenees, Edward Stourton, Doubleday UK

Detachment W: Allied soldiers and airmen detained in Vichy France 1940-1942, Derek Richardson, Paul Mould Publishing UK

Double Mission: R.A.F. Fighter Ace and SOE Agent Manfred Czernin, Norman Franks, William Kimber & Co. Ltd.

Escape through the Pyrenees: The author's wartime escape through occupied France to Spain, John Leonard Dunbar, W.W. Norton

Foreign Fields: The Story of an SOE Operative, Peter Wilkinson, I.B.Taurus Publishers & Co. Ltd.

Free to Fight Again: RAF Escapes and Evasions 1940-45, Alan W. Cooper, Pen & Sword Aviation

Growing Up in a War, Bryan Magee, Pimlico Publishing

HMS Tarana: In at the Deep End, Ron Stephens, Sue and Andy Parlour, Serendipity Publishers,

Horned Pigeon: the great escape story of World War 2, George Millar, Cassell Military Paperbacks

La Vie en Bleu: France and the French since 1900, Ron Kedward, Penguin Books,

Life Without Ladies, Major Colin Norman, Whitcombe & Tombs Ltd.

MI9 Escape and Evasion 1939-1945, MRD Foot and JM Langley, The Bodley Head, London,

Mission Accomplished: SOE and Italy 1943-45, David Stafford, The Bodley Head London

Par Les Nuits les plus Longues, reseaux d'evasion d'aviateurs en Britagne 1940-1944, Roger Huguen, Ouest France

RAF Evaders: The Comprehensive Story of Thousands of Escapers and their Escape Lines, Western Europe, 1940-1945, Oliver Clutton-Brock, Bounty Books

Receipt for a Dead Canary, Elizabeth Lucas Harrison MBE, Kindle Edition

Safe Houses are Dangerous, Helen Long, William Kimber & Co. Ltd.

Saturday at MI9: History of Underground Escape Lines in NW Europe in 1940-45, Airey Neave D.S.O., OBE, MC, Hodder & Stoughton

Secret Flotillas: Clandestine Sea Operations to Britain 1940-1944, Brooks Richards, Casement Publishers

Secret War Heroes: Men of the SOE, Marcus Binney, Hodder & Stoughton

Shadow Knights: The Secret War Against Hitler, Gary Kamiya, Simon and Schuster

Shot Down and On the Run: The RCAF and Commonwealth aircrew who got home from behind enemy lines 1940-1945, Air Commodore Graham Pitchfork, The Dundurn Goup Toronto

Silent Heroes: Downed Airmen and the French Underground, Sherri Greene Ottis, The University Press of Kentucky

Survival Against All Odds, Sunday 8th June 1942: Shot Down Over France, John Misseldine with Oliver Clutton-Brock, Grub Street Publishing

The Brenner Assignment: The Untold Story of the Most Daring Spy Mission of World War 2, Patrick K. O'Donnell, Da Capo Press

The Happy Hunted, Brigadier George Clifton D.S.O., M.C., Cassell & Co. Ltd.

The Italian Resistance, Tom Behan, Pluto Press,

The Long Walk Home: An Escape Through Italy, Peter Medd, John Lehman Ltd.

The Pendulum and the Scythe, Ken Marshall, Air Research Publications

The Price of Patriotism: SOE and MI6 in the Italian Slovene Borderlands During World War II, John Earle, The Book Guild Ltd.

The Second World War, 'In War: Resolution, In Defeat: Defiance, In Victory: Magnanimity, In Peace: Goodwill', Winston S. Churchill and assistants, Cassell & Company Ltd.

The Tartan Pimpernel: He exchanged his cassock for the cloak and dagger of the Resistance, Donald Caskie, Fontana Books,

The Women who Lived for Danger: The Women Agents of SOE in the Second World War, Marcus Binney, Hodder & Stoughton

They Have Their Exits, Airey Neave D.S.O., O.B.E., M.C., Isis Publishing Ltd.

We Landed by Moonlight: The secret RAF landings in France 1940-1944, Hugh Verity D.S.O. and bar, DFC, Crécy Publishing Limited

World War 2: The Definitive Visual Guide, From Blitzkrieg to Hiroshima, Richard Holmes (Editor), Dorling Kindersley

OTHER SOURCES

National Archive sources: TNA file WO208/3328,MI9/S/P.G./LIB/245, HS9/1232/1, CS99525, WO208/3307, 216631, HS9/1362/2, 22666/A.

The Internet has been invaluable; I have been able to build family trees on Ancestry and then find living relatives through LinkedIn and Facebook; all those I sought out willingly gave their permission for me to write about their family members.

So many people have generously given me information and I cannot be certain that they have always acknowledged the original source of the text. I can only apologise if I have inadvertently quoted any text without permission to do so.

ND - #0338 - 270225 - C0 - 234/170/11 - PB - 9781910500583 - Matt Lamination